From Chinatown to Every Town

From Chinatown to Every Town

HOW CHINESE IMMIGRANTS HAVE
EXPANDED THE RESTAURANT BUSINESS
IN THE UNITED STATES

Zai Liang

UNIVERSITY OF CALIFORNIA PRESS

University of California Press
Oakland, California

© 2023 by Zai Liang

Library of Congress Cataloging-in-Publication Data

Names: Liang, Zai, author.
Title: From Chinatown to every town : how Chinese immigrants have
    expanded the restaurant business in the United States / Zai Liang.
Description: Oakland, California : University of California Press,
    [2023] | Includes bibliographical references and index.
Identifiers: LCCN 2022030907 (print) | LCCN 2022030908 (ebook) |
    ISBN 9780520384965 (cloth) | ISBN 9780520384972 (paperback) |
    ISBN 9780520384989 (epub)
Subjects: LCSH: Chinese restaurants—United States. | Chinese
    restaurants—New York (State)—New York. | Immigrants—United
    States. | Chinese Americans—United States—Social conditions. |
    Chinatowns—New York (State)—New York.
Classification: LCC TX945.4 .L53 2023 (print) | LCC TX945.4 (ebook) |
    DDC 641.5951—dc23/eng/20220817
LC record available at https://lccn.loc.gov/2022030907
LC ebook record available at https://lccn.loc.gov/2022030908

32   31   30   29   28   27   26   25   24   23
10   9   8   7   6   5   4   3   2   1

For Catherine, Andrew, and Olivia

Contents

List of Figures   ix

List of Tables   xi

Acknowledgments   xiii

1. Introduction   1

2. Job Search: From Immigrant Networks
   to Market-Based Institutions   16

3. Making the Connection: The Story
   of the Chinatown Bus   38

4. Choices for New Immigrant Destinations   60

5. New Businesses in New Places:
   Adaptation and Race Relations   84

6. The Ties That Bind: Between Chinatown
   in Manhattan and New Immigrant Destinations   112

7. Conclusion   134

Appendix A: Methods   149

Appendix B: Analysis of Job Locations   152

Notes   159

References   175

Index   193

List of Figures

1.1. Conceptual framework   8

1.2. Map of China   9

2.1. Chinatown in Lower Manhattan   17

2.2. Detailed map of Chinatown   18

2.3. Employment agencies in Chinatown   20

2.4. Employment agencies by borough   21

2.5. Distribution of job locations in the United States   35

3.1. Map of Chinatown bus routes   43

4.1. Distribution of jobs at the phone area code level   71

5.1. Spatial distribution of business owners in six states   85

5.2. Anti-violence rally in Philadelphia   109

6.1. Printing companies and restaurant supply shops in Chinatown   117

6.2. A printing company in Chinatown   119

6.3. A cookware shop in Chinatown   120

7.1. Changes in the Chinese population in two Chinatowns
in New York City   144

List of Tables

2.1. Distribution of Chinese Hometown Associations (HAs) in the United States   29

2.2. Number of HAs of Selected Chinese Provinces in US Cities/States   30

3.1. Distribution of Daily Bus Routes by Bus Company   41

3.2. Distribution of Bus Routes by Destination State   42

4.1. Descriptive Statistics of Variables Used in the Analysis   69

4.2a. Distribution of Jobs at the Area Code Level (Survey 1: 2010)   70

4.2b. Distribution of Jobs at the Area Code Level (Survey 2: 2011)   70

5.1. Socio-demographic Characteristics by Zip Code   87

5.2. Descriptive Statistics of Business Owners   88

B.1. Estimated Coefficients from Negative Binomial Models of the Number of Jobs in an Area Code Zone   156

B.2. Estimated Coefficients from Multi-level Model of Monthly Salary (logged)   157

B.3. Estimated Coefficients from Spatial Models of Salary (logged) at the Area Code Level   158

Acknowledgments

This book has been long in gestation. The initial idea for this project emerged in the mid-2000s when I encountered a couple of employment agencies while doing fieldwork in Manhattan's Chinatown for another project. I had one of my research assistants collect job information from these two agencies for further consideration. Doug Massey's 2008 book *New People in New Places* prompted me to reorient my thinking and write a grant proposal. I want to thank the Russell Sage Foundation for the research grant (2010–2013) that has allowed me to carry out a much more systematic study of the spatial dispersion of low-skilled Chinese immigrants. I am also very grateful to the Russell Sage Foundation for the visiting scholar position that gave me the time to start the book manuscript based on this project. During my year at the Foundation, I had the opportunity to share my ideas with several fellow visiting scholars who were gracious and supportive. I am especially grateful to Ann Morning, Richard Alba, Philip Cook, and James McCann for their input which stimulated my thinking in developing this project. I also presented portions of this book at Princeton University, the CUNY Graduate Center, Queens College, the University of Pennsylvania, Brown University, and the University of Texas at Austin. I thank the participants in these sessions for their questions, comments, and suggestions.

I am very fortunate and grateful to have had a team of outstanding graduate students and collaborators who contributed to the success of this project. Simon Chen has been working with me from day one, has led the fieldwork in six states, and also conducted additional fieldwork during COVID-19. Simon speaks the Fuzhou dialect and has a passion for research. In traveling along with him on field trips, I have seen that Simon is a natural ethnographer who is adept at putting study subjects at ease during interviews. Numerous other graduate students participated in this project at different stages, including Bo Zhou, Yuanfei Li, Qian Jasmine Song, Zhen Li, Jiejin Li, Han Liu, Fenglan Chen, and Feinuo Sun, who all contributed to the success of the fieldwork, data collection, and data analysis. Yuanfei Li and Libin Fan helped with formatting and references.

Many people in the Chinese immigrant community in Chinatown provided critical help with the project. Mr. Shanren Huang (chief editor of *Chinatown* magazine), Mr. Sinhuang Cheng, and Jerry Jian Cao of the *World Journal* introduced me to many community and immigrant organization leaders, owners of Chinatown bus companies, and immigrant entrepreneurs in Chinatown. I also want to thank Mr. Sinhung Cheng, Kenneth Cheng, and David Wang for sharing their business experiences and insights on Chinatown and the Chinese restaurant business.

The State University of New York at Albany provided an ideal and supportive environment for completing this book. Two grants from the University (a Presidential Research Award and a FRAP Award) supported additional fieldwork in New York City. I want to especially thank Angie Chung, Glenn Deane, Steve Messner, Tse-Chuan Yang, Sam Friedman, Peter Brandon, and Erin Bell for their support and encouragement. Glenn, in particular, collaborated with me on a paper that eventually became one of the chapters of this book. Joanna Dreby kindly offered much appreciated guidance with regard to book publishing. The book benefited from the counsel of several immigration scholars. Doug Massey and Victor Nee provided advice at the early stages of this project. Portions of this book were reviewed or listened to by Philip Kasinitz, Nancy Foner, Chenoa Flippen, Emilio Parrado, Charles Hirschman, Dudley Poston Jr., Amy Hsin, Pyong Gap Min, Helen Marrow, Victor Nee, Dina Okamoto, Holly Reed, Michael J. White, Yao Lu, Katherine Donato, Audrey Singer, Jackelyn Hwang, Kim Ebert, Nadia Flores, John Logan, Min Zhou, and Yu Xie. As I recall, during a seminar at the CUNY Graduate Center, Phil and Nancy remarked that I "was onto something important," which boosted my confidence and energy level so that I could see this book through. Eric Moeller tirelessly edited earlier drafts and also provided sustained encouragement and advice. Brian McManus edited the entire manuscript at a later stage with care and dedication. At the University of California Press, I want to thank Naomi Schneider for her faith in the project from the very beginning and for her unyielding support, and Summer Farah for providing timely help during the review and publication process. Catherine Osborne did a superb job in the final copy editing of the entire manuscript. Stephanie Summerhays and Jon Dertien provided important guidance during the production stage. My gratitude also extends to five anonymous reviewers who provided extremely insightful comments and suggestions which have improved this book immeasurably.

Finally, I want to thank my wife Catherine, my son Andrew, and my daughter Olivia for their patience, sustained love and support, and laughter at the dinner table. Olivia's constant reminders and inquiries as to my book's progress clearly helped push me to the finish line! This book is dedicated to my family.

1 Introduction

Lisa Zheng is a thirty-eight-year-old immigrant from rural Fujian, China. She came to the United States in 2004 and married her husband not long thereafter. With the help of their parents, they started a large buffet-style restaurant in Corpus Christi, Texas, in 2006. Now, they employ fourteen restaurant workers: five Mexicans, three local whites, and six Chinese immigrants. The employment agency they use to find Chinese workers and the company from which they order their restaurant's menus are both located in Manhattan's Chinatown. The mayor considers theirs to be the best Chinese restaurant in town and dines there frequently, all the while reminding them not to hire undocumented immigrants.

Guan Chen, a thirty-five-year-old immigrant from rural Fujian province, came to the United States in 2000. In 2009, with the help of a friend, he and his wife started a takeout restaurant near a GM factory in Dayton, Ohio, and worked hard to endure through the 2008 global financial crisis. Like the Zhengs, they also rely on Chinatown businesses for such things as restaurant equipment, menus, and job recruiting. Guan still uses an accountant from New York and often returns there for personal reasons, such as weddings and medical appointments.

Chinese immigration to the United States has a long history. The 1880 US census counted 105,465 Chinese in the United States,[1] and in subsequent decades, several major cities such as San Francisco, New York, and Chicago became the major destinations for Chinese immigrants. In fact, many previous scholars have used Chinatowns in various American cities as research sites for the study of Chinese immigrants.[2] The heavy concentration of studies on Chinatowns reflects the fact that historically, Chinatowns in the United States have been the main residential and work locations for many earlier Chinese low-skilled immigrants, who often found work in Chinese restaurants, laundromats, dry-cleaners, grocery stores, and Chinese souvenir shops.

However, in the past two decades there has been a fundamental shift in the settlement trends for low-skilled Chinese immigrants towards non-traditional destinations and rural areas, driven by the expansion of Chinese restaurants in the United States.[3] By some accounts, the number of Chinese restaurants has reached more than 40,000, greater than the numbers for McDonald's, Burger King, and Wendy's combined.

A 2014 *New Yorker* article noted that there is one Chinese restaurant in Old Forge, New York, which has a population of only 756.[4] In fact, Pekin Noodle Parlor in Bur, Montana, boasts of being one of the nation's oldest Chinese restaurants, having been in operation for more than a century.[5] The immigrant business owners mentioned at the beginning of this chapter are just two examples of entrepreneurs who have not located in expected places with large concentrations of Chinese immigrants, but in faraway places such as Dayton, Ohio, and Corpus Christi, Texas. The stories of Lisa and Guan draw our attention because they are very different from the typical story of Chinese restaurants located in America's Chinatowns, where significant numbers of Chinese immigrants concentrate. Instead, the two locations are far from any concentration of Chinese immigrants or Asian immigrants in general.

The moment we learn the spatial locations of these restaurants, a whole set of questions arises as far as managing the restaurant work. How do they recruit workers? How do they manage to get restaurant supplies? How do they handle their daily lives (such as housing, seeing a doctor, religious life, raising children) in an environment where there are few other Chinese immigrants? A careful reading of these two stories gives us a hint. For example, both Lisa and Guan use employment agencies in NYC's Chinatown to hire restaurant workers, thus maintaining a continuing economic linkage with NYC's Chinese community. Moreover, they also order Chinese restaurant menus from printing companies in Chinatown. In Lisa's case, it is also interesting to observe that she also employs five Mexican workers and three local white workers. Thus, her enterprise is also building some connections between Chinse immigrant workers and other members of the community, an experience that is certain to facilitate the immigrants' adaptation to their new environment.

To understand the resettlement process of Chinese immigrants to new locations, we need to first understand the expansion of the Chinese restaurant industry. The growth in numbers of Chinese restaurants has been taking place at a spectacular speed. The industry has spread all across the United States in both rural and urban areas and large and small towns. This rapid growth and expansion did not happen accidentally, but rather as a result of multiple forces operating in concert. This book tells the story about this shift in migration patterns among low-skilled Chinese immigrants, from traditional settlement in large cities in the United States to rural and small-town locations in America's heartland. It is a story about immigrants who venture into these faraway places to open new restaurants, but also a story of workers who are willing to leave friends and social networks in New York City to find employment in these restaurants.

For scholars of immigration, this shift in spatial settlement patterns is somewhat unexpected and perhaps even counter-intuitive.

Conventional wisdom about migration often informs us that migrants tend to settle in locations where earlier immigrants had settled.[6] It should be noted that historically, some Chinese immigrants were making a living in some of the locations that we consider new immigrant destinations today. Examples are James Loewen's (1971) study of Mississippi Chinese and Huping Ling's (2004) portrait of Chinese in St. Louis during the late nineteenth century.[7] They provide important insights helping us understand socioeconomic pathways and race relations in new immigrant destinations historically. Today's spatial dispersion of Chinese immigrants is qualitatively different, as reflected in the demographic scope of this dispersion, the involvement of different institutions, and social and economic networks maintained with New York City's Chinatown.

Broadly speaking, this new pattern of spatial diffusion of immigrants is not limited to the case of Chinese immigrants alone but is occurring among other immigrants in the United States as well. For example, in 1990, 34.5 percent of all recent immigrants in the United States settled in California, as compared to only 18.95 percent in 2010. For Mexican immigrants, the story is even more striking. In 1990, 60.66 percent of recent Mexican immigrants went to California, whereas only 27 percent of recent Mexican immigrants settled in California in 2010. A similar pattern is observed for Asian immigrants as well, as 37 percent of recent Asian immigrants could be found in California in 1990 as compared to only 25 percent by 2010. These findings are based on data from the decennial US Census.

Using data from the American Community Survey for 2001–2017, I make a more detailed analysis of broad spatial patterns pertaining to recently arrived low-skilled Chinese immigrants. I rely on the diversity index, a measure of spatial pattern of immigrant settlement in fifty states and the District of Columbia. The diversity index equals 0 when all Chinese immigrants reside in one state and equals 100 when Chinese immigrants evenly distribute across all states. I report diversity index values for three years (2001, 2007, and 2017). The diversity index for Chinese immigrant restaurant workers was 59 in 2001 and rose to 68 in 2008. It rose further to 75 in 2017. When we broaden the scope to include all low-skilled workers (immigrants with education less than or equal to high school), we observe similar patterns (with a diversity index of 57 in 2001, 64 in 2008, and 66 in 2017), with a slightly lower diversity trend as compared to restaurant workers. This new pattern of the spatial diffusion of immigrants is important for several reasons. First, as compared to traditional destinations, the new destinations do not have immigrant organizations and religious institutions with personnel who speak immigrants' native languages. These two major institutions have been known to facilitate the immigrant assimilation process for many decades. In addition, immigrants who pursue the American dream in new destinations often lose access to immigrant social networks that are critical for adaptation in American society. Second, immigration scholars are also concerned that immigrants in new destinations often confront uncertain prospects regarding race relations, given that local residents in new destinations have little experience with immigrants.[8] Finally, since this spatial diffusion is taking place at a time of rising use of technology and social media, it provides some new opportunities to identify emerging empirical patterns and develop new theories to understand the spatial settlement of immigrants. As I will demonstrate later in this book, just as in the case of transnationalism that connects immigrant origins and destinations, the rising popularity of new technology (including new social media platforms) allows immigrants and entrepreneurs in new destinations to maintain linkages with immigrant organizations and churches in ways that were unthinkable only a few years ago.

Not surprisingly, the dramatic shift in settlement patterns has stimulated increasing research in this direction. Massey and Capoferro suggested four explanations for this diversification of settlement patterns. The first factor focuses on the effect of the Legalization Program from the Immigration Reform and Control Act (IRCA) of 1986 that resulted in the saturation of the labor market, especially in California. IRCA allowed nearly 3 million undocumented immigrants to receive permanent resident status in the United States. The second factor is the passing of Proposition 187 in 1994, which made California a less welcoming environment for immigrants.[9] The third factor is the "selective hardening of the border" that deflects immigrants to other destinations. However, immigrants also have a choice to move to other states once they cross the border. Nevertheless, they seem to settle in new destinations, at least for a while. The final factor is the changing geography of labor demand as a result of the restructuring of production. Significant factors include the deunionization of the workforce, subcontracting of labor (outsourcing), and the relocation of plants to non-metropolitan areas to avoid unions. As a result of this restructuring, jobs become less attractive to native workers and immigrants become a reliable and flexible substitute workforce.[10] Several studies provided evidence that is consistent with this perception.[11] In the case of California, Light's recent work points to the role of the increasingly expensive local housing market in California, which is less affordable for recent immigrants.[12]

In sum, previous studies have clearly documented the patterns of geographic diversification among recent immigrants and have advanced several explanations for these trends. Much of this work centers on the experience of Mexican and Latin American immigrants (with the notable exception of Flippen and Kim's contribution).[13] In fiscal year 2007, 41 percent of immigrants came from Latin American countries and 34 percent came from Asian countries.[14] It is important to see if there is a story, perhaps a different story, of geographic diversification for Asian immigrants. Building on this body of recent literature, this book focuses on the geographic diversification of recent Chinese immigrants.

I contribute to the current literature in three ways. First, I study the relocation of both employers (Chinese restaurant owners) and employees. In particular, I aim to identify the underlying forces that drive the diffusion of low-skilled immigrants to non-traditional destinations. In sociology, there has been a long tradition of studying immigrant spatial settlement.[15] However, this spatial assimilation model tends to look at spatial assimilation within a more or less confined environment, often in a city or major metropolitan area. In the context of immigrants moving to new destinations (often in different states), we need to broaden our theoretical scope to move beyond the vision of one single city or metropolitan area. Second, in the traditional spatial assimilation model, this residential settlement is assumed to be determined mainly by individual-level factors such as income, occupation, and race, among others. I suggest that the extant literature often directly engages in comparisons of immigrants in traditional and new destinations without a clear understanding of how and why this transition to new destinations has happened in the first place. Given the long distances to some of the new destinations and the challenges immigrants often face, I must consider other important players in this settlement process. In our case, these are Chinatown employment agencies and Chinatown buses. Third, I will explore the consequences of settlement in new destinations for employers, employees, and for the future of the immigrant labor market in the United States.

THE BASIC ARGUMENT OF THE BOOK

Figure 1.1 summarizes the logic and key components of our conceptual framework. The starting point for this framework is the diffusion of Chinese immigrant-owned businesses (mainly Chinese restaurants). The logical flow starts from left to right and the direction of arrows points to the logical link between factors. Sometimes, the logical link has one direction; at other times the logical links can go both ways and the factors reinforce each other. For example, the transportation network facilitates formation of a national labor market, and the national labor market further demands improvement of the transportation infrastructure.

I argue that this process was initially driven by the saturation of the Chinese restaurant market in New York City, which has been a

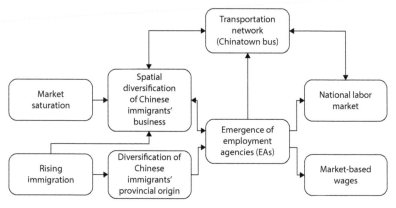

Figure 1.1. Conceptual framework of the book.

job machine for generations of Chinese immigrants. In addition, this time period also saw a major rise in immigration from China's Fujian province, creating a new supply of eager laborers (see figure 1.2).[16] Historically, immigrants from China mainly came from the province of Guangdong (Canton). However, the 1990s saw a decisive shift in this pattern. Although the exact number of newly arrived Chinese immigrants is difficult to estimate because a substantial portion of this low-skilled immigrant population from Fujian province is undocumented, estimates from the Fukien American Association suggest about 800,000. On the other hand, a survey of migrant-origin households in China suggests a smaller number of emigrants, roughly 400,000. The true number of Fujianese immigrants in the United States is probably somewhere in between. What is clear is that the large number of immigrants from Fujian has gotten notice. The topic of Fujianese immigration has been covered by leading newspapers and other magazines such as the *New York Times*, the *Economist*, and the *New Yorker*, among others.[17] The supply of this large number of immigrants provides the demographic backdrop for the diffusion of Chinese immigrants into non-gateway destinations.

By the time many recent Chinese immigrants arrived in New York in the 1990s, there was no longer an abundance of places to open

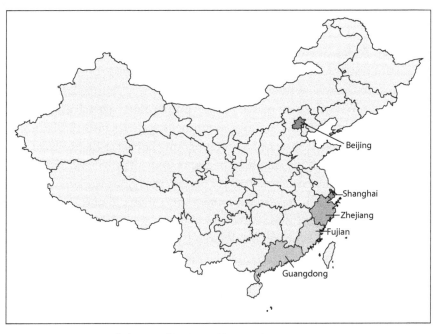

Figure 1.2. Map of China, indicating Fujian Province.

new Chinese restaurants in the city. In addition, commercial rents shot up in the 1990s, which did not help. At the same time, some immigrant entrepreneurs (who had arrived earlier and already accumulated substantial financial capital) saw opportunity elsewhere in the country. Although entrepreneurs have capital and an ample supply of labor, they still face other challenges. One of these is how to make sure they have enough Chinese immigrant workers to staff their businesses in new destinations. Traditionally, the immigrant job search process depends on friends and hometown origin-based networks. As migrant-sending origins gradually expand within Fujian province and spread to other provinces, this immigrant network-based job search process is weakened and becomes less effective. Thus, a new market-based job search process came into being in the form of employment agencies in Chinatown.

In their discussion of the nineteenth-century spatial settlement patterns of Irish and Italian immigrants in the northeast United States, Portes and Rumbaut highlighted the role of recruitment agencies during the canal construction process.[18] Likewise, Boswell also points to the role of railway companies in moving Chinese laborers from the West Coast to inland areas.[19] Employment agencies (EAs) in Chinatown differ from these recruitment agencies historically in that EAs are created by Chinese immigrants but serve the needs of everybody, including Chinese immigrants from all provinces, and in recent years, increasing numbers of Latino immigrant workers. The second challenge is how to get immigrant workers to new destinations. Since most of these recent immigrants do not speak English well, Greyhound is not an ideal option. To fill the need, immigrant entrepreneurs ended up starting their own bus companies.[20] This is the first time in American immigration history that immigrants created their own long distance inter-city transportation infrastructure.

The central argument of this book is the following. Spatial diversification was initially driven by both the market saturation for Chinese restaurants in New York City and rising Chinese immigration. At the same time, spatial diffusion of immigrant entrepreneurs generated demand for the creation of employment agencies and transportation infrastructure (mainly for immigrant workers). The emergence of employment agencies (EAs) is a market-based response to two major forces. In addition to the spatial diffusion of Chinese immigrant-owned businesses, there is another force, namely the increasing diversification of places (provinces) of origin for Chinese immigrants (to be elaborated on in chapter 2). The creation of employment agencies and inter-city transportation infrastructure further accelerates the process of spatial diffusion of Chinese entrepreneurs and immigrant workers.

In turn, this process has strong implications for individual immigrants and the formation of a national labor market for low-skilled Chinese immigrants. For the average low-skilled Chinese immigrant, I expect that a market-based job search process will more likely lead to success than the traditional migrant network-based job search process. At the level of immigrant business operation, the formation of a broad immigrant labor market has given rise to the establishment of national supply chain networks and an immigrant-based transportation infrastructure (such as Chinatown buses). Conversely, the national supply chain networks (to be discussed in detail in chapter 6) and transportation system further strengthen and expand the broad labor market for Chinese immigrant workers. The remainder of the book provides necessary details and empirical evidence for this central argument.

This book relies on three sources for its data. First, I carried out two surveys of employment agencies in 2010 and 2011. I obtained information on 2147 jobs and 2316 jobs for 2010 and 2011 respectively. I also conducted fieldwork in six states (Florida, North Carolina, Ohio, Pennsylvania, Texas, and Virginia). My research team and I did in-depth interviews with six immigrant entrepreneurs in each state and these entrepreneurs also completed our pre-designed questionnaires. Since 2010, we have also interviewed a variety of immigrant workers and entrepreneurs of various kinds as well as community leaders. Interview subjects include immigrant workers who used the services of employment agencies, owners and staff members of employment agencies and Chinatown buses, church leaders, and a social media We-Chat group leader. Detailed information on the data sources can be found in Appendix A.

In chapter 2, I introduce an important player in the process of job relocation to non-gateway destinations by reviewing the evolution of employment agencies in Chinatown. Based on a survey of employment agencies and interviews with employment agency staff and owners, I identify two factors behind the emergence of employment agencies: the diffusion of Chinese restaurants to non-gateway destinations and the increasing diversity of Chinese immigrants in terms of province of origin. I use innovative methods to gather data to support our arguments. I also discuss pros and cons of EAs from the immigrant workers' perspective. Compared to a traditional migrant network-based job search process, employment agencies make possible a market-based job search process. One major advantage of this is that immigrant workers have a much wider choice of jobs in terms of location and type of work. Another key advantage is that a market-based job search process means that workers can terminate the job if they are not happy. This is different from a network-based job search process in that a job obtained from a relative or friend from the homeland can be difficult to terminate because of the social connections involved. A key disadvantage of findings jobs from EAs is that very often jobs are located outside of New York City and transportation may be a major challenge.

I therefore provide a comprehensive discussion of the Chinatown bus story in chapter 3, where I analyze how Chinatown buses came into being and examine the critical functions they serve in helping Chinese immigrant workers and local Chinatown businesses. EAs are doing a great job of providing information on jobs across the United States and Chinatown buses help make the connection with immigrant workers. However, Chinatown buses are also drawing attention, receiving negative publicity such as reports of safety and traffic accidents and parking issues in the neighborhoods where they load and unload passengers. Although Chinatown buses began as a convenient means of transportation for immigrant workers, today their clientele is comprised mainly of non-Chinese passengers. The story of Chinatown buses shows that immigrants can create jobs in faraway locations while also building their own transportation networks. In the process, the development of an immigrant transportation network has had the unintended consequence of serving the travel needs of a much larger population who seek low-cost public transportation.

Chapter 4 examines the determinants of destination choices for restaurant owners. I explore factors to consider when immigrant entrepreneurs select a location for business operation. I approach this from two perspectives. One is through interviews with selected entrepreneurs. Second, I use data from our survey of employment agencies to explore factors that are conducive to the decision-making

process regarding immigrant business locations. Findings from both
the survey and interviews with immigrants form a coherent story
of how business locations are selected. Ultimately, business owners
strive to find locations with *haoqu*, which translates to areas with
high employment rates and low crime rates (but not necessarily the
most expensive areas). What is surprising is that, unlike what migration network theory would predict, the locations of new Chinese
immigrant businesses are not related to the locations of large populations of Chinese and Asian immigrants.

In chapter 5, I discuss what it is like to operate businesses in non-
traditional immigrant destinations. I focus on three aspects of the
consequences of doing businesses in non-traditional destinations:
the business climate and the recruitment of workers, race relations,
and family/social life. The major finding reported by business owners
is that an advantage of doing business in new destinations is that
there is less competition as compared to doing business in traditional
immigrant destinations such as New York City. I also find that business owners in new destinations are more likely to hire non-Chinese
workers (that is, Latino and white workers). Latino and white workers
from local areas are often praised by business owners for greater job
stability, as compared to Chinese immigrant workers. Doing business
in non-traditional destinations has also led to new patterns in race
relations. Some are happy stories and others are less so.

Chapter 6 is entitled "The Ties That Bind: Between Chinatown
in Manhattan and New Destinations." Given the large number of
Chinese restaurant owners establishing businesses in locations away
from New York City, the question is: what does this mean for the
traditional Chinatown in New York City? Do immigrants and entrepreneurs in new destinations continue to maintain business and
social ties with the NYC Chinese community? Chapter 6 explores
these kinds of questions. The simple answer is that despite the spatial relocation, the connections are still there. For example, Chinese
immigrant entrepreneurs continue to rely on New York employment
agencies to recruit immigrant workers. But beyond that, I can still

find other ties that bind these far-away business operations with Chinatown. I identify the following dimensions that show continuing linkages: business supplies (cookware, cash registers, surveillance systems, and menu printing); personal and business matters (weddings of friends, medical appointments, tax return preparation, and immigrant hometown association celebrations); and religion.

The final chapter engages two lines of scholarly literature. One deals with new immigrant destinations and the other with the ethnic economy. Although the spatial diffusion of Chinese immigrants is similar to that of other immigrants, the mechanisms of this discussion in the context of Chinese immigrants are quite distinctive, as outlined in the theoretical framework in figure 1.1. The second linkage is the dialogue with the literature regarding ethnic economic enclaves. Earlier discussion of how an enclave economy leads to predictions of different fortunes for business owners and employers seems to be very relevant here. For immigrant business owners, the new business model of Chinese immigrant entrepreneurship allows Chinese entrepreneurs to succeed following a different path. Instead of attaining higher education and joining the mainstream economy, Chinese immigrant entrepreneurs (most of whom are not highly educated) can also realize the American dream (run their own business, live in a middle-class neighborhood, and send their children to high-quality schools). I need to add, however, that for immigrant workers, the story may be a mixed blessing. On the one hand, immigrants working in new destinations clearly benefit more financially. On the other hand, challenging mental health-related issues (stemming from separation from friends and family in NYC) deserve more attention.[21]

Maintaining business ties is important for immigrants to successfully operate their businesses in new destinations. But perhaps more importantly, the sustained linkage helps Chinatown's vibrant ethnic economy to continue to thrive. Needless to say, the Chinatown buses facilitate this process. It is also eye-opening to observe that this linkage also takes on a new form in the context of the twenty-first century technology.

Although many immigrants and entrepreneurs left their churches in New York City, their religious faith and linkages with NYC are being maintained in other forms, chief among them various We-Chat groups. This platform is easy to learn and of no cost to immigrants. These We-Chat groups often include one leader from New York and numerous other members spread across the country who engage in frequent interactions and discussion on various topics, such as the Bible and issues affecting immigrants' lives.

The story of new immigrant destinations actually goes beyond simply making a living in new places. It actually challenges our conventional wisdom about the nature of labor markets for low-skilled workers. It is often taken for granted that the market for low-skilled workers is a local one. This book's message is that we need to revise this thesis. The Chinese immigrant story we learn from this book reveals that the labor market for low-skilled Chinese immigrants is more than local and increasingly broader and more national. In fact, this national labor market is sustained by a market-driven job search process and an immigrant-made transportation infrastructure.

2 Job Search

Most visitors to America's Chinatowns will see predictably familiar souvenir shops, endless lines of restaurants, Asian grocery stores, and vegetable and fruit vendors on the sidewalks. They are also often dazzled by signs in Chinese and English in the storefronts. The same is true in New York City's Chinatown, but if visitors venture into the alleys deep within, they will see something else, meant not for tourists but for immigrant workers: employment agencies (EAs). By my accounting, there are at least thirty EAs in Manhattan's Chinatown alone (see figure 2.1). Unless otherwise noted, "Chinatown" in this book refers specifically to this historic neighborhood in lower Manhattan that borders the Lower East Side to the east and Little Italy to the north. This is to remove any ambiguity, as we might designate at least three Chinatowns in New York City alone: one in Manhattan, the second in Flushing, Queens, and the third in Sunset Park, Brooklyn.[1]

The characteristics of Chinese immigrants in Chinatown have changed a lot in recent years. Earlier settlers arrived mainly from

16

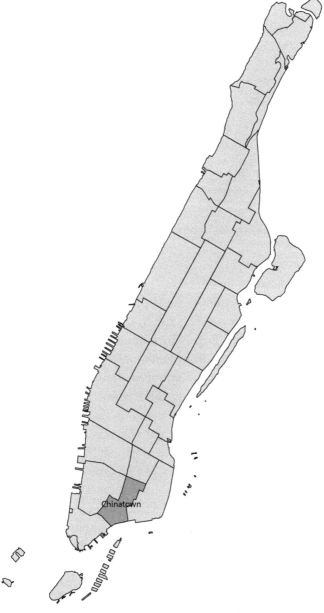

Figure 2.1. Chinatown in Lower Manhattan.

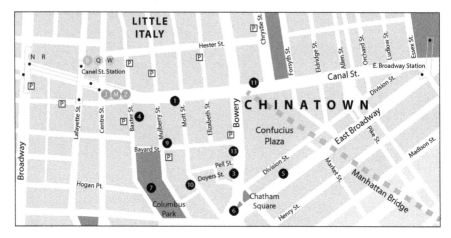

Figure 2.2. Detailed map of Chinatown in Manhattan.

Guangdong (Canton) province and spoke Cantonese or Taishanese. More recent arrivals are dominated by immigrants from Fujian province. In Chinatown, businesses run by Cantonese immigrants (and their descendants) are largely in different geographic areas than those run by immigrants from Fujian. Most tourists will visit one part of Chinatown, which is Cantonese-dominated. The two parts of Chinatown are divided along the Bowery (see figure 2.2). West of the Bowery is Cantonese-dominated Chinatown. The Fujianese-dominated Chinatown is a triangular area bordered by Canal Street (on the north), the Bowery (on the west), and East Broadway. EAs are located primarily in the parts of Chinatown occupied by Fujianese immigrants.

The emergence of employment agencies in Chinatown is significant because it is a sign of a transition from an immigrant network-based job search process to a market-based job search process. Traditionally, Chinese immigrants and other immigrant groups have consistently relied on immigrant networks in the job search process.[2] Writing in the 1990s about immigration in New York City, Waldinger stated, "getting a job remains very much a matter of whom you know. Hiring through social networks conveys significant advantages for workers and managers alike."[3] Now, however, Chinese immigrants more commonly use the service of EAs in Chinatown. How this came to be is the focus of this chapter.

FROM NETWORK-BASED JOB SEARCHES TO MARKET-BASED JOB SEARCHES

Until quite recently, newly arrived immigrants from Fujian province tended to settle in the Fujianese-dominated part of Chinatown, especially along East Broadway. Some have even dubbed East Broadway "Fuzhou Street." Indeed, it is the Fuzhou area in Fujian province and the surrounding counties from which most low-skilled Chinese immigrants now come.[4] The overwhelming majority of EAs are conveniently located in this part of Chinatown to meet the employment needs of these new immigrants. Figure 2.3 shows the distribution of EAs in Manhattan's Chinatown in this study.[5] Eldridge Street now has the highest density of EAs in Chinatown, though this very same street in the Lower East Side used to see thousands of Eastern European immigrants in the late nineteenth and early twentieth centuries. Evidence of the evolution of Eldridge Street is particularly stark, as one side of the street hosts numerous EAs while the other is home to the landmark Eldridge Street Synagogue, one of the first synagogues built in the United States by Eastern European Jews.

EAs are not limited to Manhattan and our online search in 2016 came up with no fewer than 132 EAs in New York City (excluding some duplicated entries).[6] At this point, the lion's share of EAs is located in Queens and Manhattan (see figure 2.4).[7] In Manhattan, the vast majority of EAs are located in Chinatown, a main settlement area for low-skilled Chinese immigrants. In recent years, though, as a large number of Fujianese immigrants have settled in the area of 8th Avenue in Brooklyn, EAs have begun to emerge in Brooklyn as well. The mushrooming of EAs is not only an East Coast phenomenon,

Figure 2.3. Locations of employment agencies in Chinatown.

but a similar story has also been reported in Los Angeles.[8] As students of immigration, this new pattern of job recruitment deserves our attention and further exploration.

A typical EA location is a small one-room office. Immigrant workers can often be found near the office's entrance. Most are Chinese but there may be some Latino workers as well.[9] Inside the office, one will see a divider (with finger-thin iron bars) that separates workers and staff members. Job information is posted on a bulletin board covered with small sticky notes. These notes contain the essential information pertaining to a particular job: the location of the job (as indicated by phone area code such as 202, 518 . . .), monthly salary, and work hours. Sometimes, the employer makes the request that they not be sent workers from a specific province of China, though officially it is illegal for employers to discriminate based on workers' place of origin. Additionally, there are two or three phones inside the office.

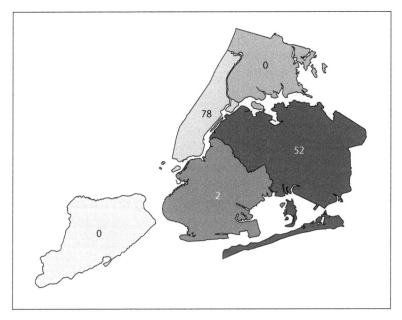

Figure 2.4. Distribution of employment agencies by borough in New York City, 2016.

A typical encounter with a staff member will start with questions such as the following: What kind of job do you want? What experience have you had? Do you have any preference regarding the job's location? If one is lucky, a staff member will immediately identify some potential jobs and start making calls. After a brief exchange, the staff member may then hand over the phone to the job seeker and an informal job interview with the employer can begin. Other times, if no appropriate jobs are readily available, the staff member will write down the applicant's information and agree to contact them at a later time.

Besides job information, staff members keep a stack of China-town bus company business cards on hand. Sometimes large posters from Chinatown bus companies can even be seen on the walls of the office. For $1, an immigrant worker can purchase a bilingual brochure with a map of the United States. However, this map is very different from a regular map one might find in a local AAA branch: this map includes all US telephone area-code coverage zones overlaid with other important geographical locations. The moment an immigrant worker finds a job, they can immediately identify the job's location on the map and get information about which Chinatown buses can take them to that particular location. Interestingly, the other side of the brochure lists frequently used English phrases, which comes in handy for addressing the basic language needs of immigrant workers. The EA thus becomes an important player in an immigrant's job search project not only for the job itself, but for navigating the journey there across unfamiliar geographic and linguistic territory.

EMPLOYMENT AGENCIES IN CHINATOWN

My investigation of EAs in Chinatown begins with interviews conducted with EA owners. In our interviews with owners of selected EAs, all noted that the first person to start a Chinatown EA was Jackson Lee, an immigrant from Guangdong Province, although no one could say exactly when.[10] In a 1994 report on a case against Lee, however, *New York Times* reporter Jane Lii implies that Lee's EA business started in 1969.[11] This time frame is broadly consistent with the information from our interviews.

Mr. Yang

Mr. Yang operated an EA business from 1997 to 2010. The day we made an appointment to interview him in the summer of 2019, he came to the meeting late and apologized, saying he "just came back from a tango dancing class." It was on this light note that we started our conversation. Dressed in a red polo shirt, Mr. Yang is a retired immigrant entrepreneur in his early seventies and looks to be in good health and high spirits. Yang, who is from Fujian province, came to the United States in 1973, when he was in his twenties, via Hong Kong. When he first came to the United States, he went to visit an employment office run by Jackson Lee. But staff members only spoke Cantonese, not the Fuzhou dialect (Yang's own native dialect). Eventually, a relative helped him get a job working for a restaurant in New Jersey. During our conversation, he frequently mentioned his business motto: "This is a capitalist society. The harder you work, the more reward you will get." His career path shows different jobs at Italian, French, Greek, and Chinese restaurants. Eventually he decided to open his own restaurant and when his daughter grew up and got a job, he decided to retire in 1997. When he retired from the restaurant business, a friend mentioned to him that it could be profitable to run an employment agency. Yang speaks good English and knows a lot of people in Chinatown. So, he started his EA in 1997 on Eldridge Street. It is a one-man operation. He sits in the office every day taking phone calls from restaurant owners across the country. Describing the earlier days of his business, Yang said, "I put ad in the Chinese language newspapers such as the *World Journal* and when business owners saw the ad, they will call me to list their jobs in my office. I did not charge employers for this service and only charged for workers who got the job. I worried that if I take money from business owners then potential workers may suspect there might be some collusion between his EA and business owners." Having said that, Yang also lowered his voice and mentioned to us that when he needed the services of employment agencies for his own restaurant (before his retirement), he actually gave some small amount of money to the EAs from time to time, just to make sure that the employment agency would find good workers for him.[12]

Doing a good job as an EA requires maintaining a delicate balance between workers and employers with the goal being to make both sides happy. On the one hand, if employers get good workers from the EA, they will be likely to use this service again. Yang stressed, "the fact that employers rely on me for identifying workers means that they trust my judgement for qualifications of workers." Sometimes, when an employer is particularly demanding, Yang tries not to make too much of an effort to find workers for them because the workers will be likely to complain. From the workers' perspective, getting a good job from Yang's EA means they will likely come back the next time they need to look for a job.[13]

The relatively peaceful and harmonious years reflect the context of the immigrant labor market in the 1990s: immigrants needed the jobs more than employers needed the workers. In recent years, however, there has been an uptick in reports of worker disputes with staff members in Chinatown EAs.[14] I asked Yang how to deal with disputes of this nature. Yang stressed that to do a good job running an EA, one must have a good heart. He said that, just like running a restaurant, you need to build a group of workers who always look for you when they need to change jobs. It is important to find a good match and it is also important to think from the workers' perspective. Restaurant workers trust him, so he has to find reliable workers for the employers. One time, a worker with a gambling problem lost all of his money and wanted to get a job but had no money to pay fees. Mr. Yang got him a job and told him to pay the fees when he had the money. Sometimes, he also has to think from the perspective of employers. If he sees any immigrant jobseeker who does not look like a hard worker, he does not introduce him or her to any employers.

Before Chinatown buses became common, Mr. Yang had to help with arranging transportation. This often meant spending ten to fifteen minutes on the phone with Greyhound bus staff, using his English-language skills to make sure that he and the immigrant worker would know exactly how to reach the worker's destination, including any transfers. Yang cited one example: "One time, after getting a job offer, an immigrant worker said, 'I do not know how to get to the Greyhound bus station.' I looked at my watch, it was after 6 p.m., I said let me take you to the bus station. I even asked Greyhound bus staff to have a stop in Chinatown to pick up some passengers with English difficulties, they said no."

Wendy Wong's Sincere Employment Agency

I also visited Wendy Wong's Sincere Employment Agency. This happens to be the agency that the New York Times reported on in 2011.[15] This EA is located in a place that does not have a high density of EAs. It is right below the Manhattan bridge and adjacent subway line. When we first started the project, the research team went to nearly all of the EAs that we could find. One reason for this was to identify how likely the owner/staff would be to allow the research team to carry out the survey we planned. Sincere Employment Agency is one of those that we visited once. Both staff members were very friendly, and as long as they were not too busy, they were happy to talk to our research team. Among all EAs that are currently operating, this EA has a rather long history. Wendy's EA is also different from other EAs in another respect. While staff members who work in other EAs tend to speak the Fuzhou dialect and Mandarin, Wendy and her staff speak Cantonese.

Wendy who appears to be in her sixties, says she started her EA business in the 1980s after having met Jackson Lee. Initially Wendy primarily helped Cantonese-speaking immigrants to get jobs outside of New York City. After all, at that time, most low-skilled Chinese immigrants were from Guangdong. Then, gradually, immigrants from Fujian and other places began to request her services. Right now, 50 percent of the customers visiting Wendy's office come from Fujian province, with the balance made up of Chinese immigrants from other provinces along with sizable numbers of Latino workers. Wendy's story shows us the evolution of the customer base from Cantonese-speaking immigrants in earlier times to Fuzhounese-speaking immigrants today.

Wendy said that these days anybody can open an EA, since few or no credentials are needed. But when she started her EA, it was a lot harder, and one had to speak English very well. The major challenge for immigrant workers then was to find the right means by which to travel. Three choices were available: (1) riding a Greyhound Bus,

(2) asking restaurant owners to come to New York City to pick them up, or (3) taking an airplane, which is the most comfortable but is generally too expensive. Although there was one notable case when a restaurant owner in North Dakota came to New York to pick up an immigrant worker, Greyhound was usually the best option. At that time, the first thing Wendy did once she secured a job for a worker was to call Greyhound to confirm details of the various bus stops. Wendy showed me some of the earlier documents from her archives. There was a stack of paper with old Greyhound schedules from different years, detailing routes from New York City to different places in the country. Furthermore, Wendy keeps a bundle of cards showing the Greyhound bus stop locations for the most frequent worker destinations. Wendy's point was to demonstrate how important it is to know English.

I also asked Wendy about recently reported disputes between immigrant workers and EA staff members. Her reasoning is that staff members are probably not always clear regarding the real working conditions, such as how long the hours are and how hard the work is. She said when a deal is reached, she always records everything on a piece of paper with information on the employer's name, location, phone number, work hours, and compensation. With this system in place, she can refer back to her notes if there is a disagreement between employer and worker. I noticed another difference between Wendy's EA and other EAs in Chinatown. Other EAs always have a divider that separates workers from EA staff members, but there is no such divider in Wendy's EA. Staff and workers can talk face to face, which certainly fosters confidence between EA staff and workers, ultimately benefiting both parties.

So far, my discussion of these two EAs indicates that both owners saw opportunities for the growth of EAs as an industry. Perhaps they did not quite realize that they were responding to the significant increase in low-skilled Chinese immigrants coming from different provinces of China, especially from Fujian province. I also note that while the EA serves a critical function by providing job information, it also facilitates employment for immigrant workers who must travel to new immigrant destinations. In earlier years, this was done by making calls to Greyhound, though nowadays it happens by means of arranging Chinatown bus service to job locations.

TWO DRIVING FORCES OF EMPLOYMENT AGENCIES

As stated in the introduction, I argue that there are two major factors behind the emergence of employment agencies. One is the increasing diversification of Chinese immigrants, and the other is the spatial diffusion of Chinese immigrants in the United States.

The Increasing Diversification of Chinese Immigrants

In 2015, the US Census Bureau reported that China had replaced Mexico as the number one immigrant-sending country, as measured by migrant flow.[16] The more than 150,000 Chinese immigrants who came to the United States in 2012 were recorded in the American Community Survey of 2013.[17] In 1990, there were 681,000 Chinese immigrants in the United States, and by 2000 that number had nearly doubled, reaching 1.2 million. By 2019, according to ACS data, there were 2.4 million Chinese immigrants, which is probably an underestimate: a significant number of undocumented Chinese immigrants are often not counted in the official data.[18]

To most casual American observers, all Chinese immigrants are the same, or are at least not that different from each other. In reality, however, there are significant variations between the Chinese immigrants we observe today and those of thirty or forty years ago. Most Chinese immigrants in the United States before 1965 came from Guangdong Province in southern China and spoke Cantonese.[19] They typically settled in Chinatowns in major cities and either worked in restaurants and laundry businesses or ran grocery stores and gift shops.

Today immigrants from China are fundamentally different and represent much broader origins—an immigration trend that has been recently reported on by National Public Radio.[20] In April 2016, the humorist Calvin Trillin, a longtime *New Yorker* contributor, wrote a poem complaining that Americans could not keep up with the different Chinese regional cuisines. "Have they run out of provinces yet? / If they haven't, we've reason to fret."[21] The poem may have been intended as innocent and humorous, but it actually created something of a global controversy, drawing commentators from both the United States and China into a debate.[22] The English edition of the influential *Global Times,* a newspaper published in China, ran its own poem, which began: "Have they run out of xenophobia?"[23]

The Trillin controversy aside, the mainstream media clearly takes notice of the unmistakable immigration story: immigrants from different provinces and regions of China to the United States are becoming increasingly diverse. For scholars, the challenge is to document this diversification systematically. Using the federal data collection system, we can obtain information on Chinese immigrants from the decennial US census, the American Community Survey, and administrative data from the US Department of Homeland Security. But none of these data sources identifies Chinese immigrants' province of origin. To overcome this challenge, we decided to use data on Chinese immigrant hometown associations in the United States, on the assumption that a higher number of HAs for immigrants from certain provinces in China represents a larger volume of immigrants from these provinces. Though this approach is not without its limitations, it does give a sense of the trend of changing statistics regarding migrant-sending provinces of origin.

Table 2.1 shows recent changes in Chinese immigrant hometown associations in the United States.[24] The top panel reveals increasing provincial diversification over time in four major immigrant locations: New York City, the District of Columbia, California, and Texas. In 1965 in New York City, for example, three Chinese provinces were represented among Chinese immigrant hometown associations. By

Table 2.1   Distribution of Chinese Hometown Associations (HAs) in the United
States by Year

| Year | Number of Chinese provinces represented by HAs in selected US cities/states | | | |
	NYC	DC	CA	TX
1965	3	0	1	0
2000	12	11	14	6
2010	15	21	22	10
2015	23	28	26	16

| Year | Number of Chinese HAs in selected US cities/states | | | |
	NYC	DC	CA	TX
1965	12	0	2	0
2000	33	9	18	4
2010	47	22	36	9
2015	130	36	57	19

SOURCE: Liang and Zhou, "The Rise of Market-Based Job Search Institutions," Table 1.

2015, New York City HAs represented twenty-three provinces in China (out of thirty-one). Similar findings are revealed for Chinese immigrant HAs in Washington, DC, California, and Texas. The lower half of table 2.1 shows the total number of Chinese HAs serving immigrants in each location. We identified twelve HAs in 1965 in New York City; again, these represented immigrants from three provinces of China. In addition to comparing HAs across time in New York City, it is informative to make comparisons between cities. Compared to New York City HAs, for example, HAs in Washington, DC, represent more provinces in China (twenty-eight versus twenty-three). But this is only part of the story: New York City in 2015 had 130 HAs, nearly four times the number in DC, suggesting that

Table 2.2   Number of HAs of Selected Chinese Provinces in US Cities/States
by Year

	NYC	DC	CA	TX
From Fujian				
1965	1	0	0	0
2000	4	2	2	1
2010	6	3	2	1
2015	75	3	2	2
From Guangdong				
1965	9	0	2	0
2000	11	0	3	1
2010	12	1	4	1
2015	13	2	4	1
From Zhejiang				
1965	0	0	0	0
2000	4	0	3	0
2010	6	1	7	0
2015	8	1	8	1

SOURCE: Liang and Zhou, "The Rise of Market-Based Job Search Institutions," Table 2.

Chinese immigrants in the DC area may be more diverse, despite there being many more Chinese immigrants in New York City than in Washington, as is consistent with the official account.[25]

Table 2.2 gives us more detailed information on how the change in HAs differs by province of origin. First, let us compare Guangdong and Fujian Provinces, using New York City as an example. In 1965, clearly the most prolific immigrant-sending province was Guangdong, which was represented by nine HAs in New York City, compared to only one representing Fujian. By 2015, the picture had changed dramatically: now there were seventy-five Fujian-based

HAs, compared to only thirteen Guangdong HAs. At the same time, the number of HAs representing immigrants from Zhejiang Province (located in coastal China) had increased significantly in both New York City and California (see figure 1.2 for locations of migrant-sending provinces).

Chinese immigrants from different provinces speak different dialects and are often embedded in their own networks. Even among immigrants from Fujian Province, a person from one town who runs a restaurant and needs to hire a worker might not know that someone from another town in Fujian is looking for a job. Thus, a Chinese restauranteur from Fujian Province, unable to staff his restaurant from his own small network of friends and relatives, has to look beyond it. In this case, the traditional network-based job search process has reached its limit. A different version of "the weakness of strong ties" is at work here: job information and choice are limited for those immigrants who know only the job availability of those within their own province-of-origin network.[26]

The Spatial Diffusion of Chinese Immigrant Entrepreneurs

In addition to the diversification of Chinese immigrants' provinces of origin, we can also observe the spatial diffusion of Chinese immigrant entrepreneurs. Here, I report results from a survey of eleven employment agencies that was carried out in Manhattan's Chinatown in 2011.[27]

Before discussing the findings from this survey, I give a brief overview of the history of EAs in New York City. Mr. Yang, the EA owner interviewed above, remembers that the fee for EA services was $100 when he was in the business in the 1990s (today's price of $30 to $40 reflects the fierce competition among current EAs.). Although earlier EAs primarily provided services for immigrants from Guangdong, over time the number of EAs has expanded dramatically; now they cater mainly to immigrants from other provinces, such as Fujian, and areas of northeast China. One key difference is that owners of EAs today are primarily immigrants from Fujian Province, because most Chinese restaurant owners in New York City and especially new destinations are Fujianese immigrants.

Perhaps the most sociologically interesting function of EAs is their insertion of market mechanisms into the settlement of immigrants. The traditional way of employment/settlement is more kinship/relative-based (that is, immigrants work for relatives or relatives' friends), and thus, exploited workers cannot complain or relocate.[28] The introduction of EAs has fundamentally changed this reliance on relatives by providing more choices in terms of job location, type, and salary scale because all job-related information is posted on the EAs' bulletin boards. Jobs in non-gateway destinations may look especially attractive because most employers provide room and board, whereas jobs in New York City restaurants provide only free food.

However, despite the attractive offer of room and board for work in non-gateway destinations, our interviews with Chinese immigrant workers reveal that they prefer to work in New York when possible, to be close to their families, friends, and immigrant community. Most workers use the Chinese word "Waizhou," which literally means "outside of New York State," to describe any work locations that are not in New York City. As such, immigrant salaries in non-gateway destinations closely reflect market prices. This means that if there is a short supply of workers in new destinations, the wages are set higher to attract immigrant workers from the allure of New York. One immigrant worker we talked to lamented, "Working in these locations away from NYC sometimes feels like a prison. Life is between restaurant and apartment. No fun and no freedom." Tina, another immigrant from Tingjiang in Fujian province, is a single mom with a child in China. She came to the United States in 2007 and works in a buffet restaurant near Yellowstone National Park. Her job is to take care of the buffet counter. She described her experience by saying,

> When I first got this job, I was offered $1800 a month and later I got paid $2400 a month. Day in and day out, I cut fruit and put it on the

fruit bar and move other food items from the kitchen to the buffet counter. Back and forth and back and forth. I also wash the restroom after all customers leave. The job is very repetitive and a lot of walking during the day makes me very tired every day. I only went to Yellowstone National Park and Las Vegas; all other times I just work in the restaurant. Life is very boring and the only place I can go locally is the mall. I got a few wedding invitations from friends and relatives in NYC. But I do not speak English and am afraid of taking airplanes. I just want to make some money to support my son's education and support my own parents.

While it is true that all workers get free room and board, this is definitely nothing fancy. Tina continues, "The boss rents a house with four rooms. He divided each bedroom into two single rooms. Sometimes there are as many as eight people staying there, all Chinese. The Mexican workers do not stay here."

There is one more reason some workers do not like to work in non-gateway places. There is a perception among immigrants, some of whom do not have legal documentation, that ICE (Immigration and Customs Enforcement) personnel often check legal papers for businesses in these locations. In contrast, both New York City and New York State have the reputation of being friendly to immigrants, both legal and illegal. There are many reports in the Chinese media that undocumented Chinese immigrants in new destinations are being taken away from restaurants and some have been deported back to China.[29]

Of course, not every immigrant thinks the same. On a sunny day in the summer of 2018, outside of an employment agency in Brooklyn, I met Brian, who has a lot of experience working in "Waizhou." Brian is taking a few weeks of vacation and came to the employment agency to see his friend. Our conversation started with the topic of where he prefers to work, New York City or Waizhou. Brian said he likes to work outside of New York City because the room is free. He added that Waizhou has better air quality, but the food quality is not as good as in New York City. "Of course, if the truth be told," he added, "any NYC job ad will be taken instantly, I just cannot get it." But Brian agrees with others that restaurant work is quite brutal and punishing. "For the first few years in the US I did not even take a day off because I had to pay the debt fee for my trip to the US. Now I have to take a break once in a while, I do not want to die before I can spend my money," Brian said.

For our survey, we obtained all of the job listings from the EAs we surveyed—over two thousand jobs in total. All of these jobs were in businesses owned by Chinese entrepreneurs. Most were in restaurants (serving both Chinese and Japanese food). For the most part, job applicants were Chinese immigrants, but some Latino workers also used the services of Chinese EAs. Just as in high-end restaurants in Los Angeles, there is a hierarchy among restaurant workers in Chinese restaurants, where Latino workers tend to work mainly as busboys.[30] Brian has a good knowledge of how restaurant culture works. He said, "Chefs are typically ranked at the top because they are often the highest paid employees. But the kitchen is very hot and feels like living in a steamer the whole day. Owners often give family members or the most trusted workers the job of receptionist because often they handle money. Receptionists also need to speak good English and take care of take-out orders. If you speak good English, server is a good choice and you always work in places with air-conditioning (unlike the kitchen). People at the bottom are busboys (who clean and wash dishes) or kitchen helpers (who prepare meats and vegetables for the chefs). It takes at least a year to move from a busboy or kitchen helper position to chef."

Besides the hierarchy within a Chinese restaurant, we also observed that increasingly Chinese entrepreneurs are opening Japanese restaurants, which is reflected in the job information obtained in employment agencies. In fact, in the United States Japanese restaurants are far more often run by Chinese immigrant entrepreneurs than by Japanese immigrants (except for some of the very high-end Japanese restaurants in big cities). Japanese food is trendy in the United States because it is perceived to be healthy and does not have a lot of

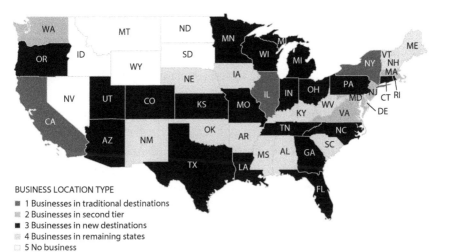

BUSINESS LOCATION TYPE
- ■ 1 Businesses in traditional destinations
- ▨ 2 Businesses in second tier
- ■ 3 Businesses in new destinations
- ▨ 4 Businesses in remaining states
- □ 5 No business

Figure 2.5. Distribution of job locations in the United States.

oil. Brian said, "unlike working in a Chinese restaurant, one must get training to be able to work in a Japanese restaurant. That training process costs money and time (about three months)." The good news for these workers, though, is that the pay in Japanese restaurants is much higher than in Chinese restaurants and working conditions are a lot more comfortable. One does not have to suffer the over-whelming heat in a typical Japanese restaurant kitchen.

For our survey, the most important job information posted at an EA was the telephone area code for each job, which located an immigrant business in operation within the geographical boundaries of that area code. Thus, this job information could be used to examine the spatial locations of immigrant-owned businesses. Figure 2.5 shows the spatial distribution across the United States of these immigrant-owned businesses in 2011. From a survey of employment agencies in Chinatown in Manhattan, we can study the spatial diffusion of Chinese immigrant–owned businesses (mainly restaurants) across the United States. In figure 2.5, we see that Chinese immigrant businesses can be found in nearly all states, with the only exceptions being Montana, Wyoming, South Dakota, North Dakota, Idaho, and Nevada. I do want to caution readers that my discussion only refers to jobs that are posted in EAs. It is possible that these states mentioned above have Chinese restaurant jobs that were not posted in EAs at the time of our survey.

One implication of the expansion of Chinese immigrant–owned businesses across the country is that the labor demand is high and constant and there are no sizable local populations of Chinese low-skilled workers to depend on. Given how widespread spatially these job locations are, even if business owners could find people in their migrant networks who are looking for jobs, there is no guarantee they would be willing to move. Thus, the recruitment of restaurant workers nationwide is better served by reliance on market-based institutions such as EAs, which can cast a much bigger net than traditional migrant networks to identify workers willing to take these jobs. The rise of EAs has had other consequences as well, such as an increase in job transitions. Gone are the days when a worker would get a job from relatives or hometown friends and stay for the rest of their life. The new normal in the Chinese immigrant labor market is that if you do not like your job, you should move on. Analysis of job histories of 410 Chinese immigrants using earlier survey in 2002 reveals that 43 percent of immigrant workers have experienced one or two job changes and 37 percent have changed jobs three or four times.[31] Second, as I will show in a later chapter, job transition leads to economic mobility, which is manifested in salary. Ultimately, the most important component to understanding the labor market regarding Chinese immigrant workers is knowing that EAs facilitate the process of spatial diffusion as it applies to such workers.

EMPLOYMENT AGENCIES AND NEW CHALLENGES

There is no doubt that EAs have filled a need to recruit workers among Chinese entrepreneurs who do business in non-traditional destinations, often far away from New York City. Yet these entrepreneurs continue to face many challenges, including those created by the development and prevalence of e-commerce.

Clearly, the emergence of EAs along with Chinatown buses (to be discussed in the next chapter) facilitate spatial diffusion of many more immigrant workers. Despite the importance of EAs, this business is encountering some challenges from e-commerce, just like any business these days. While working on this book, I continued to carry out my fieldwork on EAs in Manhattan and Brooklyn. One common complaint I have recently heard from staff members at EAs is that they face major competition from online job search companies. In fact, some of the EAs surveyed for this book are now closed, such as a few of those on Allen Street. One of the online job search companies, http://www.us168tc.com/cis, is a comprehensive online service company. Recruitment of restaurant workers is only one of the businesses in which they are engaged. Employers can now post job ads on the website for a small fee. There are several other job recruitment websites as well that are similarly structured. Clearly, the EAs are facing the challenge from online recruiting agencies. Some restaurant workers, however, do prefer the service EAs provide. Mr. Zhang, who was looking for a job at the Pingan Employment Agency in Sunset Park, Brooklyn, said he had a good relationship with staff members at that particular EA and "they are very trustworthy." In addition, if things do not work out with the employer, he can get another job without having to pay the fees again. I expect that for the foreseeable future, EAs and online job search companies are likely to coexist.

3 Making the Connection

THE STORY OF THE CHINATOWN BUS

On January 28, 2005, the *Wall Street Journal* ran a front-page article titled, "On the East Coast, Chinese Buses Give Greyhound a Run."[1] It focused on how bus companies operated by Chinese immigrants compete with Greyhound buses for customers on East Coast routes. The story took many by surprise because it seemed inconceivable that immigrant-owned businesses could compete with big name corporations like Greyhound (worth $1 billion at that time). However, underneath this sensational report lies a sociological story of recent Chinese immigration and settlement in non-gateway destinations in the United States. Located in Manhattan's Chinatown, the Chinese bus companies, also known as Chinatown buses, were created to serve the needs of recent Chinese immigrants who found jobs in Chinese restaurants. These jobs were often located far away, typically in non-gateway destinations such as Rhode Island, Maine, or Alabama. According to the *Wall Street Journal* article, these companies gained a solid footing in the business and expanded their customer base beyond Chinese immigrants due to their flexible schedules, convenient pick-up/drop off points, and less expensive bus fares.[2]

Fast forward to 2016. A decade on from the *Wall Street Journal* article, NPR reported that a group of Queens-based artists had organized a tribute (the Fung Wah Biennial) to honor the Fung Wah bus—the first Chinatown bus.[3] In fact, Chinatown buses have been quite popular among young people more generally.[4] The rise of Chinatown buses can be used as a teachable moment for immigration classes. In fact, when I teach an immigration class to undergraduate students, this is one of the topics that is often highlighted when discussing immigrant entrepreneurship. Students often raise their hands to add their own experiences with Chinatown buses, as many have taken a Chinatown bus from home to the university campus or on other journeys along the East Coast. The media has taken great interest in the Chinatown bus story as well. By my own incomplete account, those covering this topic include the *New York Times*, the *Boston Globe*, the *Philadelphia Inquirer*, the *Washington Post*, the *Wall Street Journal*, the *New Yorker* (all of which are located on the East Coast), and National Public Radio, among others.

In this chapter, I trace the brief history of the Chinatown bus's development using a variety of sources including newspaper articles, information from bus company websites, and interviews with owners of Chinatown bus companies. I argue that as Chinatown buses provide an important link between a traditional destination (New York City) and new destinations, the industry facilitates the spatial diffusion of low-skilled Chinese immigrants. I also note that because of the Chinatown bus, the model of curbside buses has been adopted by mainstream bus companies.[5] This is an important development and I argue that it provides fresh evidence of a two-way assimilation model for Chinese immigrants. Chinatown bus owners went through a process by which they learned the business of how to operate inter-city bus companies following mainstream business models. At the same time, mainstream bus companies have adopted part of the Chinatown bus business model as well: curbside parking.

THE BIRTH OF THE CHINATOWN BUS INDUSTRY

From its inception in 1997, the Chinatown bus industry has grown into a brand of its own and is a major player in the inter-city transportation market in the United States. To gauge the impact of Chinatown bus companies on the travel industry, we need to get a sense of the scale of Chinatown bus operations. I have gathered some information on Chinatown bus lines from two major websites, gotobus.com and Chinatown-bus.com, and verified some of the other companies listed on these websites. My database includes a total of thirty-one Chinatown bus companies as of 2019. Tables 3.1 and 3.2 show some basic information on Chinatown bus operations.[6] As table 3.2 indicates, the destination cities of Chinatown bus companies are no longer limited to the East Coast. Rather, these buses serve a total of 140 destination cities across the eastern United States. From table 3.1, we can see that there are roughly two categories of bus service. One group of Chinatown bus lines serves a limited number of targeted destinations. A second group is composed of much larger companies that serve a greater number of destination cities. Wanda Coach, perhaps the biggest bus company in Chinatown, serves a total of 39 destination cities with 75 departures each day. Wanda's operations are so big that the company has three bus stations in Manhattan's Chinatown (Canal Street, East Broadway, and Allen Street).

Figure 3.1 depicts the spatial patterns of Chinatown bus operations. The thickness of the lines indicates the frequency of bus service to these destinations. Clearly, the busiest bus routes are from New York City to the Washington, DC, area and to North Carolina and South Carolina, all on the East Coast. Another route goes to Midwestern states such as Ohio and Indiana. Finally, there is another important route leading to Southern states such as Alabama, Tennessee, and Louisiana. The volume of service and geographic coverage of Chinatown buses are quite striking. In table 3.2, we tabulate Chinatown bus departure schedules by state. Overall, Chinatown buses cover twenty-two states. It is quite significant to see immigrant-owned

Table 3.1   Distribution of Daily Bus Routes by Bus Company

Company	No. of destination cities	No. of bus trips	Average no. of trips
Wanda Coach	39	75	2
Atlanta Tours Inc	27	44	2
Pandanybus	20	40	2
Eastwest Bus	18	40	2
Star Line Express	21	36	2
Jaguar Bus	17	29	2
Star Line Coach	14	25	2
Eastern Bus	4	25	6
Akai Bus	22	22	1
Hibus/Rockledge Bus	3	19	6
Hi Bus Inc	4	18	5
Focus Travel	3	18	6
Lion Tickets Inc	4	17	4
Fox Bus Inc	2	14	7
Busticket Inc	11	11	1
Lionva	3	11	4
Sky Horse Bus Tour	8	10	1
Great Wall	7	9	1
Coach Run	5	9	2
Rockledge Bus	1	9	9
No.1 Bus	8	8	1
Nyth Bus	7	7	1
D&W Bus	7	7	1
Hengyun Travel	7	7	1
Tnny	6	6	1
Gd Tour Inc	1	5	5
Eastern Transport	2	5	3
Ocean Bus	4	4	1
Washington Deluxe	1	2	2
Viva Bus Inc	1	1	1
Indiana Travel	1	1	1
Total	278	534	2

SOURCE: Author's compilation.

Table 3.2 Distribution of Bus Routes by Destination State

Destination state	Destination state (abbr.)	No. of destination cities	No. of trips	Average no. of trips
Alabama	AL	10	13	1.30
Delaware	DE	3	19	6.33
Florida	FL	8	15	1.88
Georgia	GA	13	37	2.85
Illinois	IL	1	2	2.00
Indiana	IN	3	4	1.33
Kentucky	KY	2	4	2.00
Louisiana	LA	5	9	1.80
Maryland	MD	1	6	6.00
Massachusetts	MA	3	30	10.00
Michigan	MI	8	14	1.75
Mississippi	MS	1	2	2.00
New Jersey	NJ	1	3	3.00
New York	NY	7	23	3.29
North Carolina	NC	23	113	4.91
Ohio	OH	11	32	2.91
Pennsylvania	PA	7	29	4.14
South Carolina	SC	12	69	5.75
Tennessee	TN	6	20	3.33
Virginia	VA	13	77	5.92
Washington, DC	DC	1	12	12.00
West Virginia	WV	1	1	1.00
Total		140	534	3.81

SOURCE: Author's compilation.

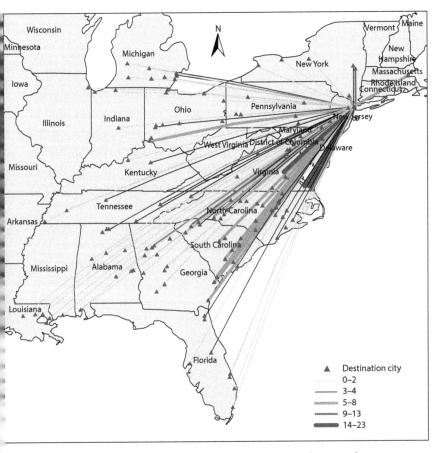

Figure 3.1. Map of Chinatown bus routes between New York City and destination cities.

bus companies serving such a broad range of geographical locations. The top five destination states (as measured by the number of cities covered by Chinatown buses) are North Carolina, Virginia, Georgia, South Carolina, and Alabama. We can also use another measure of the importance of each state in the number of daily departures. North Carolina is the uncontested leader with 113 departures each day, followed by Virginia, with 77 bus departures each day. These two states account for nearly 36 percent of all daily bus departures! This is consistent with our data collected on employment agencies, which reveals that large numbers of posted jobs are based in the Carolinas.

The large scale of today's Chinatown bus services all began with an immigrant by the name of Peter Peiling Liang, an immigrant from China who came to the United States in 1988 and took his first job in a Chinese restaurant. Liang's hometown is located in Zhuhai in Guangdong province, which is the place of origin of many earlier immigrant arrivals from China in the nineteenth century. He started an inter-city Chinatown bus company in 1997. Initially, Liang began a minibus operation that moved workers from Chinatown to Sunset Park in Brooklyn as many new Chinese immigrants were moving to neighborhoods there. While working with the minibuses, he noticed that some customers had children going to colleges in Boston who could benefit from a cheap, reliable transportation option connecting the two cities. He started the service to Boston (the Fung Wah bus) with a small number of passengers. At that time, he charged $25 for a trip from NYC to Boston when Greyhound was charging $37 each way. As his clientele began to increase, Fung Wah bus took in other passengers, often not just Chinese immigrants. One graduate student from Columbia University who started riding Fung Wah in 2002 told a reporter in 2006 that "It was really interesting to see the transition. You started seeing more and more white people coming on, black people, Indian people. It was a very eclectic mix."[7] He estimated that he had taken the bus more than a hundred times, utilizing its stop on Canal Street in Manhattan's Chinatown.

THE SPATIAL DISPERSION OF CHINESE IMMIGRANTS AND CHINATOWN BUSES

Historically, Chinese immigrants were known for building the transcontinental railroad in the United States, running laundry shops, and owning corner grocery stores. In recent years, Chinese immigrants have also become known for expanding the landscape of Chinese restaurants and for performing in kung fu movies. Ordinary Americans did not typically associate Chinese immigrants with inter-city bus transportation until quite recently. How did all this happen? How have Chinese immigrants been so successful at running these bus operations? I argue that beneath the Chinatown bus story is the larger context of rising Chinese immigration to New York City, especially from China's Fujian province. It is also an experience of assimilation for Chinese immigrant entrepreneurs who enter into the inter-city transportation business. Chinese immigrants are not the first to enter the business of transportation in New York City. After a New York transit worker strike in 1980, West Indian immigrant entrepreneurs started what is called the "Dollar Van" transportation system to provide an alternative for transporting immigrant workers to work locations around the New York metro area.[8] However, it is the Chinese immigrant entrepreneurs who were the first to operate in the inter-city transportation market.

The story behind the inception of Chinatown buses began in China's Fujian province. Located in southeastern coastal China, Fujian province historically sent large numbers of immigrants to Southeast Asian countries such as Singapore, Malaysia, and Thailand.[9] China's open-door policy, begun in the late 1970s, provided another impetus for emigration from Fujian. Some immigrants settled in Japan, but the dominant destination country soon became the United States. Much of the flow of immigrants from Fujian was low-skilled workers, often undocumented, relying on the service of "snakehead" smugglers who are paid large sums of money for arranging the international trip from China to the United States.[10] The ill-fated 1993 voyage of the *Golden Venture*, which ran aground off the shore of the Rockaway peninsula in Queens, caught the public's attention and highlighted what undocumented Chinese immigration meant in the early 1990s. However, based on a large scale bi-national survey of international migration from Fujian to New York, scholars have revealed that the tide of emigration from Fujian rose even higher in the late 1990s.[11]

As more immigrants from Fujian arrived, migrant social networks promoted further migration as earlier arrivals helped later-arriving immigrants to pay off their debts, secure housing, and find jobs. The overwhelming majority of these immigrant workers concentrated in the restaurant industry in the New York metropolitan area. As more immigrants arrived, the market for Chinese restaurants began to be saturated and new immigrant entrepreneurs who wanted to open Chinese restaurants had to think outside the box of New York City. Initially they went to nearby towns and upstate New York, but gradually, immigrant entrepreneurs ventured into faraway places such as North Carolina, Georgia, and Ohio. As more and more immigrant entrepreneurs opened restaurants in new and often distant locations, job markets for new immigrants began to change. The separation between immigrants based in New York City and these new job locations soon began to present a major challenge.

It turns out that this spatial mismatch of jobs and residential locations has been an important topic of social science research since the 1960s, mainly in the context of employment for minority group members.[12] Wilson argued that the spatial mismatch of jobs and residential locations for African Americans was one of the factors that has contributed to the spatial concentration of urban poverty they experience.[13] Much of this line of research is concerned with the distance travelled by minority workers within a major metropolitan area, but there is a similarity between African Americans and low-skilled Chinese immigrants: the spatial mismatch between residential location and job opportunities. Of course, the geographical distances demanded for these Chinese immigrants are much greater, involving not just a long-distance commute, but relocating altogether, often to different states.[14]

As the demand for inter-city travel rose, immigrant entrepreneurs came to the rescue. Peter Liang's first Chinatown bus line, Fung Wah, became the first inter-city Chinatown bus to enter the market with the aim of serving a few immigrants' need to travel to Boston. What he did not anticipate, however, was that a much bigger travel market lay ahead in the form of the large number of Chinese immigrant workers heading to jobs in faraway locations. Viewed from this perspective, the speedy development of Chinatown bus companies is easy to understand. The rise of the Chinatown bus business took place at this important juncture of the changing spatial distribution of low-skilled Chinese immigrant workers.[15]

In the early years, Fung Wah's main competition was from another Chinatown company, Lucky Dragon, which offered fares of $10 per trip from NYC to Boston. In response, Fung Wah lowered their price to $15 per trip from $25 in order to get a bigger share of the market. The two companies co-existed peacefully for a time. Fung Wah was able to retain many of their loyal passengers (such as the student from Columbia University noted earlier). At its peak, the company had thirty-seven drivers and twenty-nine buses (each with fifty seats or more).

However, this happy story did not continue for long. Starting in 2005, Fung Wah was involved in several major road accidents. One occurred in 2005, another in 2006, and still another in 2008. This series of accidents prompted a DOT investigation and the suspension of Fung Wah's license in 2013. After many attempts to renew its license, Fung Wah finally received its official renewal in 2015. However, by that time, Peter Liang had decided to close the business permanently. One reason for this decision was the lack of a bus stop in Boston. The original bus stop Fung Wah had used in Boston had been taken over by another company and an alternative bus stop was too far from Chinatown.[16]

For Chinese immigrants who travel to restaurant jobs in different parts of the country, Chinatown buses have several advantages. First, most low-skilled immigrant workers do not speak English very well. Taking Chinatown buses clearly alleviates potential language problems that could lead to unpleasant events such as getting off at a wrong bus stop. Ms. Huang, owner of the International Employment Agency (underneath the Manhattan Bridge) mentioned that before there was a Chinatown bus, she often helped Chinese immigrants navigate Greyhound bus travel. She made phone calls to Greyhound to enquire about bus schedules and she wrote down information on the destination stop as well as how to get to the bus terminal in Manhattan. However, even with help from Chinatown employment agencies, immigrants still may find it a challenge to take Greyhound buses due to the language barrier. Another impetus for Chinatown buses was that after the terrorist attacks of 9/11, airports began implementing tighter security protocols. Some Chinese immigrants, especially those without legal status, might have traveled by air before but now have to rely on Chinatown bus services. Third, Chinese immigrants like the fact that Chinatown buses tend to be faster than Greyhound buses because Greyhound buses often make many more stops before reaching their final destinations. For example, a trip to Rochester in upstate New York from New York City takes about eight hours using a Chinatown bus, whereas the same journey will take ten hours by Greyhound.

I should also note that Chinese immigrants not only depend on Chinatown buses to travel to job locations, but they also depend on them to return to New York's Chinatown for a variety of events such as wedding banquets and other social gatherings. Every year during the Thanksgiving holiday, many wedding banquets are held in Chinatown because this is the only holiday where restaurant workers can take time off. Others return to Chinatown to visit friends, attend immigrant hometown association events, or even to see medical doctors. The relatively high demand for return trips to New York for Chinese immigrants is another part of the reason for the Chinatown bus industry's success. Of course, in the final analysis, what really drove Chinatown buses to "fame" and fast expansion is that Chinatown buses have been able to tap into the mainstream travel industry by also taking passengers who are not Chinese immigrants.[17] Interviews with Chinatown bus owners often lead to the estimate that today only about 10 percent of passengers are Chinese immigrants, which is consistent with our observations during our fieldwork.

For non-Chinese passengers, there are several reasons why a Chinatown bus is a popular choice. First, bargain hunters like the Chinatown bus prices. Second, curbside pick-up has become popular. David Wang, the owner of the Eastern Bus Company, said that most people do not like going to bus terminals in midtown Manhattan because of the poor air quality and traffic congestion in that part of the city. Using Chinatown buses avoids the traffic congestion near the bus terminal. Another attractive feature of Chinatown buses is that they tend to make fewer stops between destinations compared to Greyhound buses. Finally, Chinatown buses often have more frequent departure schedules. Wang boasted that his Eastern Bus Company has more frequent departures to Philadelphia than Greyhound does.

FROM THE ASSIMILATION OF INDIVIDUAL IMMIGRANTS TO THE ASSIMILATION OF ENTREPRENEURS

Chinatown buses have gained popularity not only because they serve the travel needs of Chinese immigrants, but also because they have changed the culture of bus travel in the United States. They are inexpensive, convenient, and are often viewed as an adventurous alternative to the older, established bus lines like Greyhound or Trailways. For students of immigration, the story of Chinatown buses provides a new case for us to understand the Chinese immigration experience and to test our understanding of the assimilation process of immigrant entrepreneurs.

Since the beginning of the Chicago school of sociology, immigration scholars have been fascinated by the experiences of immigrants from different countries. One of the dominant theoretical perspectives is the assimilation paradigm, first proposed by Chicago school sociologists and further elaborated on by Milton Gordon.[18] The paradigm focuses on consensus building among immigrants, suggesting that subsequent generations become more like native or longer-established Americans. This assimilation paradigm has been the subject of many recent debates. The key argument is the idea that this uniform prediction of convergence is not quite consistent with empirical evidence, especially for some immigrant groups. Compared to the experience of earlier European immigrants, which serves as the basis for assimilation theory's testing ground, post-1965 immigrant groups are much more diverse and in most cases are non-white. Portes and Zhou proposed a "segmented assimilation" perspective to suggest alternative pathways for immigrant assimilation trajectories.[19] On the other hand, Alba and Nee continue to defend the value of assimilation perspective in the study of immigrant experiences.[20] The revised version of assimilation theory reaffirms a strong prediction from the earlier Chicago school. That is, today's immigrants continue to assimilate: as immigrants spend more time in the United States they learn English, experience mobility in climbing the occupational ladder, reside in increasingly desirable neighborhoods, and are more likely to intermarry.

Alba and Nee also stress the possibility of group convergence between immigrants and the native-born population or even two-way assimilation.[21] This latter idea has gained traction with many scholars who provide empirical cases of how immigrant groups have influenced and changed America. Orum identifies two ways in which immigrants influence American society: immigrant groups leave their imprint on the host society by taking on leadership positions in non-ethnic organizations or by using ethnic organizations to influence life outside of the ethnic community. Orum supports his theory with ample examples from Irish, Jewish, and Italian immigrants.[22] In his discussion of immigration and the "American century" (that is, the twentieth century), Hirschman identifies many components of American culture that are attributable to immigrants, from Hollywood to Broadway.[23] Diaz and Ore provide compelling evidence that Asians and Hispanics influence local expression of culture as reflected in preferred choices of cuisine.[24] Jiménez proposes a new theory of assimilation: relational assimilation, which involves "back and forth adjustments in daily life by both newcomers and established individuals. . . ."[25] Using data on second generation Asian Americans in California, Jiménez, Horowitz, and colleagues argue that in the case of educational achievement, Asian American students (not white students) set the new standard for all groups.[26] This contradicts the conventional wisdom of using non-Hispanic whites as a reference point for all studies of immigrant assimilation.

I find supporting evidence for this new revisionist assimilation perspective in the case of Chinese immigrant entrepreneurs such as Chinatown bus owners. The classical assimilation paradigm often considered that becoming an immigrant entrepreneur is, in itself, a successful outcome. Indeed, there are many books on immigration that explore the process of becoming entrepreneurs.[27] In the eyes of some scholars, however, *becoming* an entrepreneur is the measure of success—which may overlook the possibility that some immigrant entrepreneurs are more successful than others. To the extent that immigrant entrepreneurs are considered to have more control over their employment, and given that employers are often paid more than employees, it is reasonable to treat becoming an immigrant entrepreneur as an indicator of success. The reality, of course, is much more complicated. In fact, becoming an immigrant entrepreneur is just the beginning of becoming American and learning the American way to manage a business. The assimilation process of immigrant entrepreneurs is often bumpy and sometimes very unpredictable.

This is clearly the case for Chinatown bus owners. Most immigrants who are in this business are not well-educated and had no previous experience in running a bus company. Although Chinese immigrants may have some advantages in running other "traditional immigrant businesses" such as restaurants, laundries, or grocery stores, managing today's bus business entails a much more complicated process. There are regulations concerning customer safety, drivers' qualifications, bus maintenance schedules, and parking locations. All of these require a much deeper understanding of the standard American way of doing business, which is quite different from how a typical Chinese immigrant's business functions. If a Chinese immigrant opens a new restaurant, he or she can always find someone to help if there is a problem because this is a well-established ethnic business in the United States. However, this is clearly not the case for running an inter-city bus operation. Bus operations often involve a much bigger investment financially; a regular inter-city bus can easily cost over $300,000 and bus companies often own multiple buses. All of this is to say that there is a lot to learn for Chinese immigrant bus owners. Sometimes the learning curve in this new business is steep, and the assimilation process for business owners is often costly.

Another key component of the revised version of the assimilation perspective is to stress immigrants' contributions to various dimensions of American life, from arts and film to the technology industry, to, in our case, the inter-city transportation business.[28] In the following section, I analyze the development process of Chinatown buses and highlight key findings to show the value of this revised model of assimilation. I want to begin with a surprising and significant development: Chinatown buses contributed to a revival of the bus industry overall. Prior to the emergence of Chinatown buses in the late 1990s, the motorcoach business was in significant decline and bus transportation was considered to be undesirable by many potential passengers in the market. In fact, bus travel is often seen as the last resort, used by people with no other choices.[29] Chinatown bus companies created the innovative curbside model in 1997 and today, most mainstream bus companies have followed suit. This list includes Megabus, BoltBus, and Greyhound, among others. One of the biggest players in this business is Megabus, which started its US operations in 2006. It runs curbside buses from New York to Boston and other East Coast cities. Megabus's current curbside departure locations in New York City concentrate on 34th Street between 11th and 12th Avenues in Manhattan. Many universities have similar bus stops near their campuses. Travelers like this flexibility and convenience, as compared to a traditional departure location, such

as a formal bus terminal. Remarkably, the Chinese immigrant entrepreneurs' innovation has been adopted as the new industry standard
today. This has been accompanied by a steady increase in the ridership of inter-city buses. In 2008 there were 45 million inter-city bus
passengers; that number rose to 61 million in 2015.[30]

Now for the bad news. The development of the Chinatown bus
industry has by no means been very smooth. At the initial stages of
development, there was cutthroat competition among all Chinatown
bus companies. Some of the competition has been very ugly and has
occasionally involved violence, even murder. This prompted a NYPD
crackdown on crimes involving bus companies. This negative publicity also prompted the NYC Department of City Planning to carry
out a formal study of the Chinatown bus industry.[31] Indeed, things
often get worse before getting better.

Besides uncontrolled competition, safety also became an important concern. The large number of accidents that involved Chinatown
buses prompted the US Department of Transportation to require an
overhaul of the industry in 2012. To be precise, a total of twenty-six
Chinatown bus companies were shut down for investigation in 2012,
perhaps the biggest overhaul action for bus companies in US history. Only one major Chinatown bus company (holding more than
ten buses) remained open at the time. The DOT report cited evidence that Chinatown buses have an accident rate of 1.4/1000, as
compared to 0.2/1000 for other mainstream bus companies. The
DOT has cited numerous violations with Chinatown buses such as
their employment of drivers with expired licenses or who have not
been tested for drugs and alcohol; the lack of regular inspection and
maintenance of buses; and excessive overtime work for drivers.[32]

After the DOT crackdown, Chinatown bus owners did some
soul-searching and subsequently, the business of Chinatown buses
has been transformed. Now, most Chinatown bus companies follow
DOT guidelines and regulations and have re-applied and obtained
operation licenses. Today most Chinatown companies keep good
records regarding bus maintenance and drivers' time behind the

wheel. In addition, some owners of Chinatown buses merged and consolidated their businesses. For example, there were once three companies competing with each other on the New York City to Albany route. At one point, a one-way ticket could be found for as little as $8 or even $5, a price level that was clearly unsustainable. No company could generate profit operating this way, so after much discussion among shareholders, the three companies have since merged into today's JL bus company. In addition, all Chinatown bus companies cooperate with DOT regulations around driver hours. For example, if a driver has accumulated a total of fifteen hours of driving, they may not drive for at least the next eight hours. Bus drivers are also required to go through safety training offered by the DOT. Since 2018, a new ELD (Electronic Logging Device) has been implemented by the DOT instead of using a traditional paper logging system. With this new ELD system, every bus has a computer. Drivers use their licenses to log in and the moment they begin driving, the time will be recorded automatically. The DOT can easily check each driver's log if needed.

In 2012, the same year of the DOT crackdown, New York governor Andrew Cuomo also signed legislation that requires all bus companies to apply for permits for their proposed bus stops. As of 2021, most Chinatown bus companies are in compliance with this requirement. As such, anyone who takes a Chinatown bus will see a sign with the Chinatown bus company's name and travel destinations. For example, a rider arriving at Allen Street can look for a sign that says "Eastern Bus, Philadelphia, Washington DC." In the wake of the DOT overhaul in 2012, Chinatown bus ridership continues to make a resurgence. A year after the DOT overhaul, bus ridership had dropped from 4.8 million to 4.6 million. It only took a year for Chinatown buses to recover, however. The ridership for the next two years was 5.0 million in 2014 and 5.3 million in 2015.[33] This big-picture story shows, however, that learning the ropes of operating an inter-city bus service is by no means easy for Chinese immigrants.

CONCLUSION

The diffusion of low-skilled Chinese immigrants across the country has presented a new challenge for employers and employees. In the social science literature, similar issues have fallen under the umbrella of "spatial mismatch hypothesis" because of the mismatch between the locations of job growth and residences of potential individuals (especially minority group members) who need the work. This spatial mismatch among minority group members, especially African Americans, has been studied for more than four decades. The Chinese immigrant entrepreneurs confronted this challenge by creating a Chinatown curbside bus industry to initially serve the need of low-skilled immigrant workers. In doing so, Chinatown buses facilitate the process of spatial diffusion. However, this business innovation has led to a major change in inter-city transportation. For one thing, the Chinatown bus owners have found a market that is much bigger than they had anticipated. The expansion of the customer base certainly makes the business more profitable for shareholders. Since the market is so favorable, many players have tried to get involved without adequate planning and understanding of the business. Unfortunately, this rapid development initially took place at the cost of safety and also led to some violence between competitors. The Chinatown bus industry has certainly learned these lessons the hard way. Below I summarize several important points coming out of the Chinatown bus study.

First, the development of the Chinatown bus from its birth to today's well-developed industry has important implications for immigrant entrepreneurship, ethnic economy, and the future of Chinatowns in the United States. The creation of the Chinatown bus industry has taken the model of Chinese immigrant entrepreneurship to a new level. It breaks the traditional stereotype that typical Chinese immigrant businesses can only concentrate in restaurants, laundries, grocery stores, or Chinese supermarkets. Of course, we can certainly still acknowledge the value of traditional immigrant entrepreneurs in restaurants and grocery stores and their role in achieving social-economic mobility. A poster child of this mobility path is Gary Locke, former governor of Washington, whose grandparents ran a grocery store not too far from the governor's office in that state. A recent example is Jon Chu (director of the film *Crazy Rich Asians*), whose parents own a well-known Chinese restaurant in California.

Compared to traditional Chinese immigrant businesses, however, owners of Chinatown buses need to have a deep knowledge of the inter-city transportation market and the operation of the industry and its regulations. Almost by definition, financial investment in a Chinatown bus company is categorically different from operating a small restaurant. Typically it requires more shareholders to get involved. It is indeed a path-breaking initiative for Chinese immigrants to play an important role in the inter-city transportation market. For students of immigrant entrepreneurs, it is no longer sufficient to only look at the immigrant migration experience or immigrant social networks (as is often the case in studies of immigrant entrepreneurship). In this case, we must pay attention to an inter-city transportation market inhabited by bus companies and customers (both Chinese immigrants and all others). Today when we look at Chinatown bus patrons, we see a rather small percentage of Chinese immigrants or students and a majority of customers who are ordinary Americans of all ethnicities and ages. This stable customer base portends the long-term health of a sustainable Chinatown bus industry and its continuance as an important player in the inter-city transportation industry.

I also argue that the development of the Chinatown bus industry has had a significant impact on not only the future of Chinatown in Manhattan but also Chinatowns in other cities in the United States. Data from the US Census reveals that Chinatown's population in Manhattan declined from 2000 to 2010. Population decline and recent gentrification have prompted some commentators to suggest the possibility of "the end of Chinatown." However, Willington

Chen, executive director of Chinatown Development, does not agree, in part because of the customers Chinatown buses bring into the area. Chen says, "Chinatown buses [are] just like blood vessels that circulate blood throughout the human body, in that they bring all customers to Chinatown from different directions. When people are in Chinatown, they always consume something and make other purchases."[34] Chen's estimate of the economic impact of Chinatown buses is about $100 million each year. David Wang, owner of Eastern Bus, also reminded us that "there are many passengers who arrive in Chinatown late in the evening. Chances are they have not had a good meal for a while, having dinner in Chinatown is a must before going home or heading to [their] next destination." Consumption in Chinatown is of course good for Chinatown businesses.

In addition, to the extent that many Chinatown buses link China-town in Manhattan to Chinatowns in other cities (especially Boston, Philadelphia, and Washington DC), Chinatown buses also help propel Chinatown businesses in other cities. Specifically, we can see some interesting links between Chinese food and Chinatown buses. Chinese food is already well-integrated into American life, consumed by many, from soldiers in the Middle East, to astronauts in space, to actors in Hollywood movies and comedy shows. As many more Americans use Chinatown buses for their travels, Chinatown buses also become a regular part of their lives. This is particularly true for people who live on the East Coast. I opened this chapter with the story of the first Chinatown bus, Fung Wah. In 2015, Fung Wah was shut down. After many setbacks with the DOT and millions of dollars of lawyer/consultant fees, the owner, Peter Liang, finally decided to discontinue the bus service. In a world with so many bus companies, the closing of a Chinatown bus company in New York City could easily go unnoticed by the average customer. But Fung Wah was iconic enough that a musician and writer for the *New Yorker*, Marc-Philippe Eskebnazi, composed a nostalgic song entitled "Farewell Fung Wah" (imitating Bob Dylan's style) which has been posted on YouTube with over 20,000 views so far.[35] A website called "Chinatown Bus Stories" has been collecting stories from passengers and creating an anthology and a book based on these entries written by Chinatown bus travelers.[36]

Beyond its economic impact on Chinatowns in Manhattan and other cities in the country, the Chinatown bus story also informs us about the economic impact of low-skilled immigrant workers in the United States. Recent findings on the economic impact of immigration in the United States from the National Academy of Sciences suggest complementarity among highly skilled immigrants and the native-born population, but more competition among low-skilled workers.[37] For highly skilled immigrants, perhaps this is an unintended consequence of the Chinatown bus, as it taps into a travel/transportation market that has been underexploited. In so doing, it allows many consumers (especially minority group members) to travel by means that they can afford and save some money along the way. Perhaps more important economically, it helps to add new energy and directly or indirectly revitalize the inter-city transportation industry.

Returning to the literature on immigration, the Chinatown bus also has a major story to tell. For the past two decades, many immigration scholars have attempted to modify the traditional assimilation paradigm or come up with alternative theoretical perspectives to describe the experiences of contemporary immigrants. There is an increasing consensus that views immigrant adaptation as a two-way street. This trend was captured very nicely by the Social Science Research Council, which sponsored a conference in the 1990s entitled "Becoming American and America Becoming."[38] The case of Chinatown buses illustrates this argument. On the one hand, the process of the Chinatown bus's development over time shows bus company owners learning how to run major American companies, including adapting to complex national and local regulations. This is also a process of Chinese immigrant entrepreneurs integrating into the American business community. They adopt the modern management form of other companies: spend money on advertisements, make available online booking for tickets, introduce adjustable ticket prices (Thanksgiving holiday is often the most expensive ticket price) and official curbside bus stops, and provide free WIFI and other en-route entertainment for the trip. This is clear evidence of the further integration of Chinatown bus companies into the general motor-coach industry.

On the other hand, Chinatown buses' innovations have been adopted by other bus company owners. It was the Chinatown buses that first introduced the now-popular curbside bus model. Indeed, today nearly all major bus companies have adopted this business model, which has contributed to the revival of bus travel in the United States. It is fair to say that the history of Chinatown buses is an important chapter in both the transportation history and the immigration history in the United States.

4 Choices for New Immigrant Destinations

Immigration researchers have long taken it for granted that immigrants concentrate in major gateway cities and states. Historically, for many Chinese immigrants, going to the United States was almost synonymous with going to the Gold Mountain (San Francisco). Traditional settlement cities in many ways symbolize the meaning America. Well-cited seminal studies tacitly embraced and perpetuated this attribution by focusing on major metropolitan areas with large numbers of immigrants.[1] Some observed that post-1965 immigrants concentrated even more in selected locations than previous immigrant cohorts.[2]

Recently, researchers noticed an emerging phenomenon of immigrants arriving at non-traditional destinations.[3] Using data from the US Census, Singer showed that nearly one-third of immigrants resided outside of established settlement states in 2000 and subsequent studies have produced significant insights into the settlement process in new destinations.[4] However, research has focused almost exclusively on Mexican and Latino immigrants, although Flippen and Kim, who study Asian Americans, are a notable exception.[5] I argue that it is equally important to carefully examine other groups, who may reveal different patterns, so that we may consolidate, or perhaps challenge our understanding of the new settlement process. In this chapter I study low-skilled Chinese immigrants who have recently arrived in new immigrant destinations.

While acknowledging that these arguments likely hold for Chinese immigrants, I argue that the study of Chinese immigrants in new destinations brings additional theoretical and empirical significance. A major trend that characterizes recent settlement of Chinese immigrants in non-gateway destinations is that the process involves both Chinese employers (restaurant owners) and employees. Business ownership itself can be a measure of success and the expansion of Chinese restaurants to non-gateway destinations provides a new (perhaps faster) avenue for economic mobility. This expansion also challenges the consensus that ethnic economies need to remain concentrated.[6] How Chinese immigrant owners operate and adapt in such a new environment is not well understood. Furthermore, the recruitment mechanism for moving to new destinations may differ across ethnic groups. Chinese employers heavily rely on employment agencies (EAs) operated by Chinese immigrants and located within New York City's Chinatown in Manhattan. In chapter 2, I discussed these agencies' emergence in Chinatown and their operation. The EAs provide critical information to potential employees about new destinations and the employers there. Perhaps more than realized, EAs facilitate the settlement process for employees who venture into the new destinations. Thus, a systematic examination of new patterns of employment and settlement among recently arrived low-skilled Chinese immigrants is clearly needed.

In this chapter, I undertake a systematic study of the determinants of destination choices for Chinese-owned businesses and consequences for immigrant workers and entrepreneurs. Using New

York City as a research site, I join research efforts to examine patterns of settlement and assimilation among recent Chinese immigrants in non-gateway settings. I have three objectives. I pay particular attention to contextual factors that are conducive for Chinese immigrant entrepreneurs' business expansion into non-traditional destinations. I also explore consequences of the new settlement pattern for immigrant adaptation and economic mobility by focusing on linkages between immigrant wages and geographical location. Thirdly, I identify new patterns of Chinese immigrant entrepreneurship in new immigrant destinations.

CHINESE IMMIGRANTS IN
THE NEW YORK CITY CONTEXT

For a long time, researchers needed only to go to Chinatowns in different cities to study Chinese immigrants. However, this strategy no longer accurately captures contemporary Chinese immigrants in the United States. For recently arrived low-skilled Chinese immigrants, most of the employment opportunities are located outside of Chinatown. This chapter provides a more nuanced analysis of the settlement process in non-gateway destinations. I argue that this process results from the saturation of the Chinese restaurant market, which was a job machine for generations of Chinese immigrants in New York, and a corresponding increase in job demand due to a rise in immigration from China's Fujian province.[7] By the time many Chinese immigrants arrived in New York City in the 1990s, there were no longer places to open new Chinese restaurants, with some estimating that there were as many as two thousand Chinese restaurants in the region by the 2000s. In addition, commercial rent rapidly increased, which lowered the potential profit margin and further dimmed the prospects for opening new restaurants. As such, Chinese immigrant entrepreneurs face a competitive market if interested in opening their own restaurants.

UNDERSTANDING THE SPATIAL LOCATIONS OF
CHINESE IMMIGRANT BUSINESSES

Historically, ethnic businesses often have often begun by serving the needs of co-ethnic groups, either in the form of restaurants or grocery stores.[8] In this regard, the close proximity of ethnic businesses to ethnic neighborhoods was important. Ivan Light and colleagues carried out a series of studies of immigrant entrepreneurship among Korean, Chinese, Japanese, and Iranian immigrants.[9] In most cases, their studies reveal that the spatial clustering of immigrant businesses (often located in immigrant enclaves) is a key characteristic of these businesses. For example, even when Korean immigrants in Los Angles moved their businesses to the suburbs, their businesses were still spatially clustered and continued to rely on Korean immigrant workers.[10] Light and his colleagues did identify an exception: Iranian immigrant business owners in Los Angeles.[11] Iranian immigrant business owners are not spatially clustered and do not need to employ other Iranian immigrant workers, perhaps due to the very small scale of their businesses.

Recent studies of ethnic economies provide evidence that there are advantages in utilizing the ethnic social capital embedded in immigrant neighborhoods because social capital fosters and facilitates entrepreneurship. One of the challenges for immigrants starting their own businesses is accessing financial capital. Many immigrants lack the good credit necessary to obtain loans from mainstream financial institutions, so they rely on co-ethnic members to pool financial resources to start their businesses. One way of doing this is for several aspiring immigrants to co-own a business. Another common strategy is to use a credit rotation association (in Mandarin Chinese, *biaohui*). The practice of credit rotation has long been noted and continues today. The basic idea of a credit rotation association is that everyone contributes a fixed amount of money at regular intervals which is distributed to each member in turn so that each can benefit from this process.[12]

Perhaps the chief advantage of locating businesses near immi-grant neighborhoods, however, is easy access to immigrant labor.[13] Fong, Luk, and Ooka suggest that the human ecology perspec-tive predicts that immigrant businesses are likely located in a city's "transition zone," which is characterized by a high level of poverty and social disorganization.[14] However, findings from their study in Toronto are not consistent with this perspective. Another perspective draws insight from economic geography. Rooted in the new indus-trial space thesis,[15] Zhou studies the role of inter-firm networks in the location strategies of Chinese producer service firms in Los Angeles.[16] For example, Chinese-run computer businesses are typically located on the fringe of areas of heavy Chinese concentration while maintain-ing proximity with other computer distributors so that parts can be exchanged faster and more efficiently. Both studies, in Toronto and Los Angeles, note this shift in Chinese business patterns of settlement from the ethnic enclaves, such as Chinatown, toward the city out-skirts or suburban areas, clearly signaling a departure from the tradi-tional business settlement patterns. This pattern can be explained in part by the increase of Chinese immigrants living in suburban areas or "ethnoburbs."[17] There is also a fundamentally demand-side expla-nation advocated by economists that stresses the economic indicators of destination locations: unemployment rate, income level, and busi-ness climate.[18] This line of reasoning posits that entrepreneurs are more likely to open new businesses in locations undergoing economic growth with rising employment. This perspective is consistent with some of our interviews with restaurant owners as they tend to iden-tify "good locations" (*haoqu*) for their business operation.

Employment Agencies, Recruitment of
Immigrant Workers, and Chinatown Buses

Current perspectives on business location choices are not entirely satisfactory in explaining the case of Chinese restaurants. I extend the inquiry on business locations by including the establishment of

Chinese restaurants in remote places. The recruitment of workers is a critical function for any business, and maybe more so for ethnic businesses. This is typically not an issue when the business is in a traditional gateway destination because an abundant supply of immigrant workers is available. However, there is a spatial disconnect between Chinese businesses in faraway places and their supply of immigrant workers in gateway locations such as New York City. The emergence of employment agencies (EAs) in Manhattan's Chinatown fills this gap.

The current literature on non-gateway destinations rarely discusses the recruitment process for immigrants.[19] In the case of Chinese immigrants, EAs fulfill this function. For example, in the three or four blocks around East Broadway and Eldridge Street in Manhattan's Chinatown, there are around thirty EAs. These EAs are important facilitators for the settlement process in new destinations. EAs resemble labor market intermediaries or brokerages in the mainstream economy.[20] As Stovel and Shaw indicate, "successful brokerage results in the flow of some good, service, or information from one party to another."[21] The key benefits of EAs is that they save both employers and employees time that would have been spent either searching for workers or searching for work.[22] Particularly in the case of workers, they no longer need to look through job websites or newspapers every day.

In addition to serving the needs of Chinese immigrant workers and immigrant entrepreneurs, the emergence of EAs also responds to the increasing diversity of Chinese immigrant origins. Province of origin is no longer confined to Guangdong, which historically was the most important immigrant-sending province, but now include other provinces, such as Fujian, Zhejiang, and the northeast regions of China. Traditional kinship and village-based migration networks are limited in this diverse environment and market-based job search agencies can cast a much bigger net. In addition, as the number of EAs increases in Chinese communities in NYC, their inflation-adjusted fees have been reduced significantly. Mr. Yang, an EA owner in Chinatown, stated that when he first came to the United States in 1973 the fees were $30 per transaction. Today EAs still charge about $30-$35 per job transaction. This price has remained nearly unchanged for more than forty years! The current fee structure makes it easier for immigrant workers to look for or change jobs. More importantly, staff members in EAs provide needed information about non-gateway destinations and often work with bus companies to help immigrants learn how to travel to new restaurants or other job opportunities. Since they have the most up-to-date information on the restaurant job market, EA staff can also relay information about new locations and suggest routes to bus companies.[23]

Although EAs in Chinatown provide information to potential immigrant workers, there is still the challenge of the spatial mismatch. Most of the newly established Chinese restaurants are in remote places far from Chinatown and the many potential immigrant workers concentrated in the NYC area. The mismatch between jobs and workers has been a central focus of recent studies on minority groups. This mechanism was proposed as one of the leading causes of unemployment for some minority and immigrant groups.[24] For example, Wilson argues that the unemployment rate for blacks is high because of the spatial mismatch between inner city blacks and job growth in suburban areas.[25] In the case of Chinese restaurants, Chinatown buses were created to solve the spatial mismatch of jobs and employees by providing convenient transportation for restaurant workers. As such, Chinese immigrant entrepreneurs help maintain job growth by opening new restaurants and providing a transportation network to connect recent immigrants with those job opportunities.[26] As Chinatown buses continue to expand, many other minority groups, especially African Americans and Latinos, have become frequent passengers.

Perhaps the most sociologically interesting function of EAs is their insertion of market mechanisms into the settlement of immigrants. As I recounted in chapter 2, the traditional way of employment/settlement is more kinship/relative-based (that is, immigrants work for relatives or relatives' friends). In these situations, immigrants may be exploited but cannot complain or relocate.[27] The introduction of EAs has fundamentally changed this reliance on relatives, providing more choices in terms of job location, type, and salary scale because all job-related information is posted on the bulletin board of the EAs. Jobs in non-gateway destinations may look especially attractive because most employers provide room and board, whereas jobs in New York restaurants provide only free food. However, our recent interviews with Chinese immigrant workers reveal that they prefer to work in New York to be close to their families/ relatives, friends, and the immigrant community. As such, immigrant salaries in non-gateway destinations closely reflect market prices. This means that if there is a short supply of workers in new destinations, the wages are set higher to attract immigrant workers from the allure of New York.

With respect to linking wages with immigrant enclave employment, a heated debate emerged in the 1980s and 1990s about the economic benefits of working in immigrant enclaves. Portes and colleagues argue that immigrant workers in an enclave receive higher returns on education than those working outside an enclave.[28] In contrast, Sanders and Nee show that the enclave hypothesis is only true for employers.[29] Long-time Chinatown observer Peter Kwong goes further to suggest that Chinese immigrant workers are exploited by Chinese immigrant business owners.[30] I add a new spatial dimension to this old debate by looking at immigrant workers who work in a gateway city (New York) and comparing them with those in faraway locations. In both cases, the actors are still Chinese immigrants, but the job locations have changed.

Chinese restaurant chefs provide a good example of how faraway locations shed new light on the economic benefits debate. A 2009 newspaper report suggested that chefs in non-gateway locations are paid about $2,300–$2,700/month, while chefs in New York City are only paid about $2,000–$2,300/month despite the higher cost of living there.[31] Employers who offer below-market wages are less likely to receive job applications when the salary level of other job listings is known. Thus, we can expect an association between the spatial distance of jobs and the salary offered, with the farthest jobs offering the highest wages. Furthermore, job mobility is increasingly possible because immigrants can leave their current jobs for other higher-paying jobs without constraints imposed by kinship/ relatives. In remote destinations most employers are close to their employees and even provide a shuttle service for going to work. This closeness and interaction may enhance the opportunity for employees to learn business tips from their bosses, and eventually start their own businesses. Thus, the training system for entrepreneurship may work more effectively in new destinations than in New York, where an employer's main concern is that workers get their jobs done.[32] In this chapter, due to data constraints, I only test the wage differentials between immigrants working in New York City vs. immigrants working in non-traditional destinations, and I await the testing of other ideas (such as linking entrepreneurship with non-gateway destinations) in future research.

MODELING THE CHOICES OF BUSINESS LOCATION AND WAGES FOR IMMIGRANT WORKERS

Using data collected from surveys of EAs along with supplementary data from the US Census and the FBI, I aim to answer two basic questions. First, I identify important factors that affect immigrant entrepreneurs' decision to start a business in certain locations. Second, I explore the extent to which immigrant workers are paid differently by location (as measured by physical distance from Manhattan). Note that the variables of interest (including the locations of businesses) are measured at the telephone area code level. We merged job distribution data with other socio-demographic data such as racial composition, population size, median household income, unemployment rate, and crime rate. For a technical discussion of these statistical models, see Appendix B.

Table 4.1   Descriptive Statistics of Variables Used in the Analysis

Variable	Mean	Std dev
Number of jobs in area code (2010)	7.84	11.65
Number of jobs in area code (2011)	8.42	11.42
Percentage of non-Hispanic white (2010)	65.56	18.60
Percentage of black (2010)	12.71	10.66
Percentage of Asian (2010)	4.35	4.73
Population (2010)	1,469,162.00	1,065,010.00
% 2010 median household income < $40,000	9.52	29.41
% 2010 median household income range $40,000–$50,000	40.66	49.21
% 2010 median household income range $50,000–$60,000	27.84	44.90
% 2010 median household income range $60,000–$70,000	14.65	35.43
% 2010 median household income range > $70,000	7.33	26.10
Percentage of unemployed population (2005)	4.75	0.93
Property crime rate (2010)	0.02	0.01
Number of establishments (accommodation & food service)	3,016.08	2,115.15
Cost of living (2010)	930.37	282.34

SOURCE: Liang et al., "From Chinatown to Everytown," Table 1.

Table 4.1 provides descriptive information about the variables used in our analysis. Table 4.2a presents the distribution of the number of jobs in each area code from our wave 1 survey in 2010. Overall, we see that Chinese restaurant jobs spread into 64 percent of the 274 area code zones in the United States (96 area code zones out of 274 contain no jobs). Nearly 24 percent and 20 percent of area codes

Table 4.2a   Distribution of Jobs at the Area Code Level (Survey 1: 2010)

Number of jobs in the area code	Frequency	Percent
0	96	35.04
1–4	66	24.09
5–14	55	20.07
15–24	31	11.31
25–34	16	5.84
35+	10	3.65
Total	274	100.00

Table 4.2b   Distribution of Jobs at the Area Code Level (Survey 2: 2011)

Number of jobs in the area code	Frequency	Percent
0	74	27.01
1–4	75	27.37
5–14	64	23.36
15–24	36	13.14
25–34	17	6.20
35+	8	2.92
Total	274	100.00

SOURCE: Liang et al., "From Chinatown to Everytown," Table 2a and 2b.

have one to four and five to fourteen jobs listed for Chinese restaurants, respectively. Over 20 percent of area code zones are characterized by high-density job availability, which is defined as a having a minimum of fifteen jobs in each zone. Similar results are reported in table 4.2b using the 2011 wave 2 data.

Figure 4.1 shows the distribution of jobs obtained from our EA survey in New York City. Evidently, the jobs are widely distributed

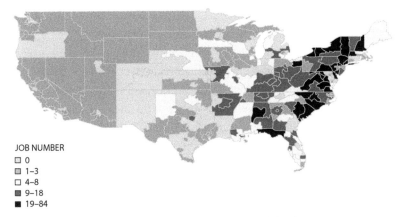

JOB NUMBER
☐ 0
◻ 1–3
☐ 4–8
■ 9–18
■ 19–84

Figure 4.1. Distribution of jobs at the phone area code level.

across the United States. We identify job frequency using different shades, with the darkest colors indicating the largest number of available jobs, and lighter colors indicating the least number of jobs. Overall, these job listings spread across thirty-seven states. There is a striking spatial pattern of job distribution. The density of available jobs declines with distance from New York and there are few jobs located near the West Coast, which seems to be a separate labor market for immigrants. Although the labor market for New York-based immigrants is largely national, it does not quite extend to the West Coast.

The map in figure 4.1 is also consistent with the classification method proposed by Massey: the Big Five, Second Tier, New Destination, and "remaining" states.[33] With Massey's classification scheme, jobs in new destinations and remaining states represent 55 percent of the job listings. This reveals a dramatic geographic diversification of restaurant job locations and a high concentration of jobs in non-gateway destinations in the United States, which as argued previously is likely facilitated by Chinatown bus companies; we found large stacks of business cards from bus companies in every EA we visited (see chapter 3 for more discussion).

In order to identify factors that are attractive to immigrant business owners as they site their businesses, I conducted an analysis of the determinants of job distribution by area code. The study used the following area code-level characteristics: median household income, unemployment rate, crime rate, proportion of non-Hispanic whites and blacks, and number of business establishments providing accommodations and food. Because the dependent variable is the number of jobs in each area code, we estimated a negative binomial model. For this model, state level fixed effects are included in Model B. Results are shown in table B.1 in Appendix B. I note that the Moran's I, a global measure of spatial autocorrelation, for Model A is statistically significant, but once we enter state-level fixed effects in Model B, the Moran's I becomes insignificant, indicating that spatial dependence has been purged from the model.

Predictions from the economic sociology of immigration and the migration networks perspective do not fare well in this study. Chinese restaurants and jobs are generally found in places with high rates of non-Hispanic whites and blacks, but not in places with high concentrations of Asians/Chinese. This is consistent with our interviews in which immigrant entrepreneurs call all locations not in New York City "waizhou." "Waizhou" connotes being far away from the Chinese immigrant community. This finding is broadly consistent with the idea that Chinese restaurant businesses in new destinations rely on EAs for the recruitment of workers because of a lack of Chinese immigrant workers locally. But does this mean immigrant networks are dead in this case? Far from it. Immigrant business networks are alive and well, but function in a new way that is not easily captured by our statistical models. Even though recruitment of workers often relies on the service of EAs in Manhattan, there are strong immigrant business networks operating to facilitate the expansion of the restaurant business in new destinations.

A Chinese restaurant owner in Virginia explained how the networks still operate in with this example. "Five years ago, my uncle was doing restaurant business in Virginia and recommended a place (about fifty miles from his restaurant). Doing business in this area, my uncle knows this place has good business (*shengyi hao*). My uncle said to me, 'If you do not come, I know someone else will.'"

Jennifer and her husband moved to Texas in 2010 to start a buffet restaurant in a small town with a total population of 20,000. It is the only buffet restaurant in town. Jennifer shares this experience:

> Before 2010, we had been running a Chinese restaurant in a black neighborhood in Philadelphia. It was long brutal hours (11 a.m. to 3 a.m.) every day. It was not a safe neighborhood at all, we were robbed more than five times. My daughter was often bullied in her school and several times her lunch box was stolen in school. She cannot stand that neighborhood any longer. My older sister started her business in Texas in 2000. After learning our business situation in Philly, she encouraged us to move to Texas. She promised to pool money (*hegu*) with me for this buffet restaurant.

The main reason for pooling money was that Jennifer's older sister knew there was a good opportunity to make a profit in that location and therefore felt comfortable contributing money to the new business. Still another restaurant owner, Jay, decided to move to Virginia after learning from his cousin (who worked for a local shipping company) that there were some good business opportunities to be found there. A broad message from these interviews is that the spatial diffusion of Chinese restaurants continues to rely on immigrant networks, defined by family, friends, and place of origin. This certainly resembles immigrant networks that we have observed in Chinatown.

In line with the business climate perspective, our statistical models show that these restaurant jobs tend to be located in areas with low unemployment rates. As restaurant owners tend to start businesses in low crime areas, the coefficient for crime rate is negative and statistically significant. In our interviews, restaurant entrepreneurs often told us that when opening businesses, they look for *haoqu* (a good community or neighborhood), which could be interpreted as having low unemployment and a low crime rate. In the idealized world, *haoqu* possesses the following characteristics. Most important is business potential (*you shengyi*, which is one of the most frequently used Chinese terms among business owners). In our statistical models, this kind of neighborhood is measured broadly by median household income and unemployment rate, which are the basis for any good neighborhood for business operation.

Different immigrant entrepreneurs try to find the *haoqu* using different approaches. For Mr. Zheng, who operates several restaurants in North Carolina, the search for a new business location started with the internet. He said, "Before I start a new business in a new location, I will look at information on the local population (whites vs. blacks), mean income, and commercial housing price. I also want to check the number of restaurants already in operation. The second step is to travel to that location to get a sense of the business community and living conditions. I also want to see what kinds of cars people are driving, to gauge the quality of this community." Some immigrant entrepreneurs take as much as two weeks to observe the community and neighborhood before making their final decisions. There is also a restaurant magazine called *Chinese Restaurant News* (中餐通讯) that regularly recommends places to open restaurants.

Based on interviews in these six states as well as with entrepreneurs in New York City, I can roughly define three categories of business owners. The first group of immigrant entrepreneurs applied a "fishing expedition" approach. They would drive from New York and look for locations that they thought might be good for business expansion. Kenneth Chen, President of the Chinese Restaurant Association, described it this way: "They would first look for locations within two-three hours of driving from New York City, that could cover places such as parts of New Jersey, parts of upstate New York, and parts of Connecticut. Then, they would expand to locations with five to six hours of driving from New York City. They often have good luck finding a place." When we interviewed staff members working at EAs, we met one woman who used to be a restaurant owner with her husband. She said that when they were looking for a place to open their restaurant, they just kept on driving until they found a location they liked.

The second group of immigrants wanting to start new businesses looked at newspaper ads to see what was available. We met Mr. Jiang in Chinatown in late 2013. He came to the United States around 2010 and had already held many jobs. His first job was as a restaurant delivery driver in Brooklyn. He described for us an incident that almost cost him his life. One time on a food delivery trip in Brooklyn, he was robbed at gunpoint by a white man who may have been on drugs. Luckily Mr. Jiang had some money in his pocket, so the robber took it and left without hurting him. He described this experience with a sense of pride and humor. He had also worked in Tennessee and North Carolina and was then ready to start his own business outside of New York. Asked why he was not interested in doing business in New York City, he said that he could not afford to buy a house for his family there and housing outside of New York is much more affordable. He read local Chinese newspapers every day, looking for prospective neighborhoods in which to settle. When noting something interesting, he would google the neighborhood to find out median household income and other demographics (such as racial/ethnic makeup). He would then travel to that location to study the neighborhood and ask questions like: Do people drive nice cars? How much business activity is going on? Of course, the most important factor to consider would be whether he thought that he could make a profit there. He would then visit a restaurant for sale in the area and observe the customer volume over the course of a few days. It turns out that this is a strategy many immigrant entrepreneurs follow when preparing to buy a restaurant in an unfamiliar location.

The third group of business owners were immigrants who had some connection with the potential locations of their new businesses. In most cases, the immigrant entrepreneurs had been employed in the area. A forty-five-year-old restaurant owner in Dayton, Ohio shared this story with us: "I arrived in the United States in 1999. In

2004, I was working for this Japanese restaurant in Dayton that was owned by a Korean immigrant. In 2010, the Korean owner wanted to retire and I decided to take over the business. The previous Korean owner told us many business tips and she is actually now working part time for me." Others took a more or less ad hoc approach. One restaurant owner in a suburb of Philadelphia explained it this way: "I have heard other friends' businesses are doing well in Philadelphia, my wife and I spent a weekend driving around the suburbs of Philly and finally found a neighborhood that we like."

We can also gain some insights by looking at the actual locations of some of these restaurants. Many restaurants are located inside big shopping malls or strip malls, which is perhaps the best way to get enough foot traffic. Other restaurant owners choose their locations near big companies. A business owner who has a restaurant in Ohio explained, "our business location is ideal because there is a big GM factory (with 100,000 workers) only three miles away, a stable customer base! Our business is at the front of a road used by all workers going to work each day. There is only one more restaurant around here, almost no competition." Another immigrant entrepreneur who operates a Vietnamese restaurant and chose a location near a military base told the same story and added that solders and military staff like his drive-through shop.

The Ohio business owner mentioned "competition." In fact, this is another issue that immigrant business owners expressed a lot of concern about. A community perceived to be a good business environment also means there is not a lot of competition from similar local restaurants, especially other Chinese restaurants. Some of the newly opened Chinese restaurants start "price wars" by offering below-market-price meals in order to attract customers. Mr. Zheng, who owns a business in North Carolina, told us that "the Chinese restaurant owners should work together and should not cut each other down (*huxiang caitai*). If we start lowering our prices below the market rate, we will all suffer in the end (*dajia douchikuei*). If the price is too low, customers will think we offer garbage food (*laji shipin*)."

Haoqu also means a good place for families to settle and to realize their American dream (for example, buying a house). One restaurant owner who moved from New York to Virginia shares his experiences with us: "My wife is not well educated (*mei wenhua*) and worked in a garment factory in New York City at the time. Our family of four paid $1600 a month at the time for a small apartment in Chinatown in Manhattan. There is no hope of buying a house in New York. I spent nearly a month thinking about where to start our business before moving to Virginia." Another restaurant owner in Virginia likes the new location as well: "this is a good environment, safe and appropriate for my children to grow up (*shihe haizi chengzhang*)." Our statistical models also confirm that safety is a major component of a good business location (as measured by crime rate) but is also important to children's development.

MOVING OUT AND MOVING UP?

I next assess how salary is related to new destinations. For this exercise, I shift attention from business owners (as measured by characteristics of business locations) to workers' salary. The substantive question is, "Do immigrants receive higher compensation once they move out of New York City?" The focal information that operationalizes this research question is a distance measure between Manhattan (area code 212) and each destination area code using area centroid points. Table B.2 (see Appendix B) reports results from the multilevel models of logged monthly salary for migrant workers. The "distance from NYC" coefficient in Model A and Model B is positive and statistically significant: as jobs move further away from Manhattan, the expected monthly salary increases. Model B further disaggregates the logged monthly salary regression by job category (cook—the reference category—server, delivery driver, and others). Surprisingly, servers are paid higher salaries than cooks. I speculate that this is because servers require English language skills to communicate with dine-in customers and to take orders over the phone. Among recently arrived, low-skilled Chinese immigrants (often with only a middle school education), this level of English proficiency is not universal and thus is rewarded. In contrast, getting training and experience in cooking skills is relatively easy.

In Table B.3 (see Appendix B), we estimate spatial models of monthly salary at the area code level. Again, results from the spatial error (Model A) and spatial lag (Model B) models support the inference that distance from NYC increases logged monthly salary. I note that although this finding of a more favorable salary for Chinese workers who live away from traditional immigrant destinations is consistent with earlier studies using ACS data,[34] the potential individual selectivity bias is minimized in this case. It is possible that Chinese immigrants with characteristics positively associated with earnings, such as high education level, ambition, or motivation, are more likely to move to new destinations. However, using the ACS to observe salary differences between Chinese immigrants who reside in new immigrant destinations versus traditional destinations does not account for these characteristics. The salary level in our data is set by employers and is not a direct function of individual-level characteristics.

So, how do we explain the rise of salary for workers in new destinations as compared to New York City? Fundamentally, this is driven by supply. Specifically, more workers want to work in New York than in new immigrant destinations. Therefore, to get workers, employers have to raise salaries. This desire to stay in New York is not hard to explain. For many low-skilled Chinese immigrants, the city is their first stop in the United States and they generally prefer to stay close to their families, friends, and people from their hometowns who cluster there. Second, the common perception among immigrants is that life in new destinations is boring for workers. The main sources of entertainment are cell phone video games and watching Chinese TV shows on the internet. One immigrant worker described working in new destinations: "[it] feels lonely, like in prison and no freedom." Immigrants may also wish to stay close to New York because they believe

that federal agents from ICE (Immigration and Customs Enforcement) regularly check workers' legal documents in some of the restaurants in new destinations, which creates a sense of fear among
immigrants without papers. One Chinese immigrant lamented, "if
you draw a line between NYC and Florida, the further away you
are, the tougher the ICE is in arresting undocumented immigrants."
Another immigrant complained that ICE officers in Texas only targeted undocumented Chinese immigrants and turned a blind eye on
undocumented Mexican immigrants.[35]

NEW PATTERNS OF BUSINESS EXPANSION IN NEW IMMIGRANT DESTINATIONS

We have documented how Chinese immigrant entrepreneurs make
decisions about business locations in new immigrant destinations
and the implications for workers, yet there are also new patterns
of business expansion in these new locations. Using several data
sources collected by our research team over the years, my colleague
Han Liu and I explored this topic in a recent work.[36] A key strength
of our data source is information on business history. We collected
detailed information on each business, including timing of business
creation, location, and size, which allows us to study the business
trajectory of immigrant entrepreneurs. Our analysis indicates that
while it can take a longer time for immigrants to establish businesses
in new destinations, these businesses are likely to expand. This finding supports our theoretical speculation that the lack of a co-ethnic
community in new destinations makes it time-consuming for immigrant entrepreneurs to look for business locations and financially
prepare for opening. However, once a business gets established, there
is less competition in new destinations than in traditional gateways.
In addition, these new destinations tend to have low commercial
rental costs. Recent developments in the ethnic-based transportation infrastructure (Chinatown buses) and supply chain factors are

also important. They keep businesses in new destinations connected to the co-ethnic support system in traditional destinations like New York City, making it possible for businesses in new destinations to order supplies online from Chinatown.[37] These factors together provide conditions that are conducive to expansion into multiple businesses. Previous research on immigrant entrepreneurship has been focusing on financial outcomes or the business owners' subjective assessment of their businesses, largely overlooking business expansion as a measure of entrepreneurial performance.[38]

These results indicate that the transition from one to multiple businesses spells a change in the model of immigrant entrepreneurship. Running a single business, in many ways, represents a survival strategy for immigrants to make a living in a new country, especially for new arrivals whose English is poor. Multiple immigrant-owned businesses, in contrast, is akin to the franchise business model used by Subway, KFC, etc., in the mainstream economy. In the case of immigrant businesses, this franchise model is often informal, but our exploratory analysis still indicates that these businesses tend to have business partners other than family members. While involvement in multiple businesses means more coordination and responsibilities than the traditional mom-and-pop model, it also indicates a new path for socioeconomic mobility.

CONCLUSION

This chapter aims to examine a new employment and settlement pattern for low-skilled Chinese immigrants in the United States. Relying on unique surveys of EAs in New York City's Chinatown, I systematically analyze this new pattern. The results show that there has been a fundamental shift in patterns of settlement among recent, low-skilled Chinese immigrants. The days of these immigrants congregating exclusively in Chinatown for jobs and settlement are long gone.

A substantial number of low-skilled jobs today are located across the United States.

This decisive shift in the employment pattern of low-skilled Chinese immigrants is due to several critical factors. First, the broad economic picture is that New York City's market has made it difficult and unappealing to open new Chinese restaurants there. A limited customer base and high commercial rent values prompt immigrant restaurant entrepreneurs to look beyond the city. Although fieldwork suggests that there have always been Chinese immigrants who ventured outside of New York City and opened restaurants in remote places, nothing compares to the scale of present-day expansion.[39] The Chinese restaurant business today has reached almost everywhere, from Alabama to Alaska. Beyond factors related to New York's restaurant market, I have argued that two more factors were critically important in facilitating this expansion: the role of EAs and Chinatown buses. EAs established market mechanisms to build a bridge between employers and potential employees. The Chinatown buses greatly reduced the transportation needs of low-skilled Chinese immigrants. With convenient routes and reasonable prices, Chinese immigrants can easily navigate across geographic spaces without a high degree of English proficiency.

The fundamental shift to non-gateway destinations has several important consequences. The trend of moving to non-gateway destinations opens up a broader labor market that can provide employment opportunities for a substantially larger number of immigrants. In this sense, the recent significant entry of immigrants from Fujian province cannot be sustained without these Chinese immigrant entrepreneurs opening restaurants in different parts of the country. Likewise, without the large supply of immigrant workers, these entrepreneurs cannot realize their American dream of starting their own businesses. This is a win-win situation for entrepreneurs and low-skilled immigrant workers. It is often the case that geographic mobility leads to socioeconomic mobility. Immigrants who choose to work in non-gateway destinations can reap a significantly higher salary than immigrant workers in New York. This echoes previous studies finding that immigrants working outside of ethnic enclaves obtain better economic advancement than those working in the enclaves.[40] Recent literature seems to give short shrift to the issue of how new destinations are linked to socioeconomic mobility for immigrants. Our study provides evidence that moving out in this case means moving up, as measured by increased salary.

Previous scholars reveal that this new settlement pattern in non-gateway destinations leads to new challenges such as a potential increase in conflicts over race and ethnic relations, especially in locations where residents have not encountered large numbers of immigrants before.[41] However, our fieldwork in Chinatown reveals that this new settlement pattern may be improving some inter-group relations. Because of the short supply of Chinese immigrant workers in non-gateway locations, entrepreneurs often rely on non-Chinese workers, especially Latino workers. To accommodate this link, there is an EA that specializes in recruiting Latino workers for Chinese entrepreneurs. To attract Latino workers, staff members in the agency display currencies from major Latin American countries, which creates a familiar and comfortable environment for the job search. Staff members also facilitate the process by using simple Spanish phases to ensure communication with potential workers. While this certainly provides employment opportunities for Latino workers, this process also raises interesting research questions as well. For example, if we follow the "training system" logic of Bailey and Waldinger,[42] Chinese immigrants working for Chinese employers are likely to become entrepreneurs themselves, thus leading to social mobility. However, it is unknown whether this training system extends to the Latino workers in Chinese immigrant-owned businesses.

Turning to the determinants of the location choices for Chinese restaurants and jobs, we find that the economic sociology of immigration, which suggests locating ethnic businesses near immigrant residential locations, was not supported. In fact, Chinese restaurant locations and jobs are strongly associated with the presence of non-Hispanic whites. This implies that Chinese business owners cater to a non-Hispanic white customer base, not other Chinese customers. This challenges the traditional wisdom that ethnic-owned businesses need to cater to other ethnic group members.[43]

This chapter also sheds light on why the expansion of Chinese restaurant businesses into vast areas in the country has been so successful. Chinese restaurant owners seem to focus on attracting relatively low- or middle-income groups as their main patrons. This strategy ultimately ensures a large potential customer market. We also find that new immigrant destinations allow immigrant entrepreneurs to expand their businesses and open more restaurants over time.

Theoretically, our study has implications for a need to (re)conceptualize the immigrant labor market.[44] Much of the existing literature tends to conceptualize the immigrant labor market as being within a city or a metropolitan area and studies how immigrants choose to work in (or outside of) an ethnic enclave or in a suburban area.[45] As Fong, Luk, and Ooka argue, the human ecological perspective, based on the early twentieth century experiences of European immigrants typically concentrated in central cities, does not explain the current spatial patterns of Chinese businesses in suburban Toronto.[46] In the case of low-skilled Chinese immigrants in the United States, this somewhat narrow conceptualization of the immigrant labor market is clearly not sufficient, as many Chinese immigrants choose to work in faraway places across the country. To study spatial locations of current immigrant businesses and workers, this chapter calls for broadening the understanding of the immigrant labor market to a wider geographic region in this country.

5 New Businesses in New Places

ADAPTATION AND RACE RELATIONS

In this chapter, I will draw on a survey and interviews with thirty-six immigrant entrepreneurs in six states to explore three sets of issues. These immigrant business owners are located in Pennsylvania, Virginia, North Carolina, Florida, Ohio, and Texas; their actual distribution is depicted in figure 5.1.[1]

The recent significant spatial diversification of immigrants in the United States has drawn attention from immigration scholars due to several factors. Researchers are interested in the business model of immigrant entrepreneurship in non-gateway destinations.[2] Much of the recent sociological literature concerning immigrant owned businesses centers on businesses in immigrant enclaves such as New York's Chinatown, Los Angeles's Koreatown, or Miami's Little Havana. Scholars have argued that such spatial concentration of immigrant owned business in these locations has major advantages, such as nearby potential customers and convenient access to immigrant workers.[3] Thus, the dispersion of immigrant entrepreneurs raises a serious question about how immigrant entrepreneurship works in non-gateway

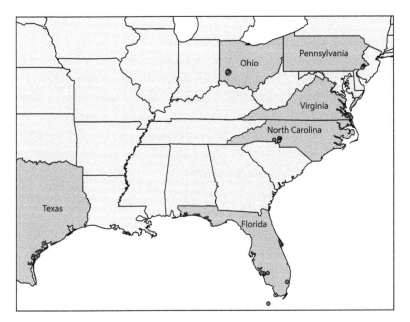

Figure 5.1. Spatial distribution of business owners in six states.

destinations. So the first set of questions is: how do immigrant entrepreneurs select business locations and recruit workers in this case?

The second set of questions concerns the social adaptation process of immigrants in these non-gateway destinations. This concern
is driven by the fact that immigrants in traditional destinations have
the advantage of easy access to major immigrant organizations and
immigrant-sponsored churches that go a long way to help newcomers settle. This begs the question of how immigrants adapt in
non-gateway destinations without access to these organizations. The
third area of interest among students of immigration, perhaps most
important sociologically, is the potential tension between immigrants and local longtime residents who have not been exposed to
large numbers of immigrants before. There has been a long history
of conflict between African Americans and minority merchants who
do business in African American neighborhoods. Earlier friction

between Jewish merchants and African American residents has been replaced by conflict between African Americans and their Korean merchant neighbors in New York City, Los Angles and other cities.[4]

In this chapter, I aim to explore these three questions. I begin with a discussion of some of the major characteristics of my interview locations in six states and profile the immigrant entrepreneurs who operate businesses in these locations. This will be followed by a detailed discussion of each of these three issues concerning immigrant entrepreneurs in new destinations.

SOCIO-DEMOGRAPHIC CHARACTERISTICS OF NEW IMMIGRANT DESTINATIONS

In table 5.1, I show major socio-demographic characteristics of neighborhoods as identified by the business owner's zip code. These are the neighborhoods where immigrant entrepreneurs were interviewed. In general, this study covers three kinds of neighborhoods across six states. Geographically, the study area contains four states along the East Coast: Pennsylvania, Virginia, North Carolina, and Florida; one in the Midwest (Ohio); and one in the South (Texas). We can also classify the study area's population by race. In this case, we see that the neighborhoods in Ohio, Florida, and Texas are primarily white, with all three above 85 percent. The neighborhood in Virginia is nearly three-quarters white. The Ohio, Florida, and Virginia neighborhoods also show very similar household income levels, in the $60,000-$65,000 range. The neighborhood in Texas is mainly a lower-middle class Hispanic neighborhood (63 percent Hispanic) with a median household income of $41,000. The neighborhood in North Carolina and the neighborhood in Pennsylvania share something in common: a high proportion of black residents coupled with a generally low income. However, the neighborhood in Pennsylvania is more extreme, with 45 percent of the population living below the poverty line. This is a neighborhood of mainly blacks

Table 5.1 *Socio-demographic Characteristics of Local Population by Zip Code, Based on 2010 to 2014 ACS data*

	TX 78411	OH 45459	FL 33966	NC 28262	VA 23455	PA 19140
Total population	27,869	27,577	8,348	41,498	49,246	53,608
Median household income (USD)	41,366	65,419	62,553	45,941	64,772	21,918
Percentage of income from public assistance	3.4	1.1	1.9	1.9	1.5	14.7
Percentage of population below poverty line	18.2	6.0	6.5	24.3	7.5	45.3
Gender (percentages)						
Male	46.9	47.8	47.1	49.5	50.1	47.4
Female	53.1	52.2	52.9	50.5	49.9	52.6
Race (percentages)						
White	85.2	88.3	87.6	37.3	74.3	15.0
Black	3.9	5.1	5.5	42.2	15.4	58.7
Asian	1.4	2.6	4.0	14.1	4.7	1.0
Chinese	0.02	1.1	2.0	1.9	0.5	0.5
Other race	9.5	4.0	2.9	6.4	5.7	25.3
Hispanic of any race	62.9	2.1	14.7	8.1	8.1	40.6
Employment (16 years and over, percentage)						
Employed	55.8	56.7	52	61.8	55.6	39.3
Unemployed	7.9	4.5	4.9	8.4	16.3	13.3
Not in labor force	36.3	38.7	43.1	29.8	28.1	47.4
Education (25 years and over, percentage)						
High school or more	83.4	95.4	94.0	93.5	94.3	67.3
Bachelor's degree or more	20.2	45.4	36.8	44.4	38.6	5.0

SOURCE: Author's compilation based on USA.com local data search.

Table 5.2   Descriptive Statistics of Business Owners

Variables	N	Mean/percentage	Std dev
Year of birth	36	1975.2	9.82
Marital status	36		
Single	3	8.33%	
Married	33	91.67%	
Education	35		
Primary school or lower	11	31.43%	
Middle school or high school	21	60.00%	
College or higher	3	8.57%	
Year of arrival in the United States	36	1996.33	6.79
Work experience in New York City	36		
Have not worked in New York City	16	44.44%	
Have worked in New York City	20	55.56%	
Total number of jobs held	36		
1	4	11.11%	
2	4	11.11%	
3	7	19.44%	
4	5	13.89%	
5	10	27.78%	
6	4	11.11%	
7	2	5.56%	
Total number of businesses owned	36		
1	22	61.11%	
2	7	19.44%	
3	2	5.56%	
4	3	8.33%	
5 or more	2	5.56%	
Number of businesses owned currently	36	1.42	1.25
Number of employees[a]	49	7.14	5.2
% of family members among employees[a]	48	32.18	32.65

a. For all businesses that were still running at the time of our project survey.
SOURCE: Author's compilation based on survey by the research team.

(58.7 percent) with a substantial Hispanic population as well. This is also a neighborhood where only 5 percent of the residents have a college degree and 33 percent did not even complete high school. This neighborhood resembles some of the poor neighborhoods studied in earlier research, such as Lee's work in New York City and Philadelphia, Min's in New York City, and Yoon's in Chicago.[5] In fact, this general area of Northwest Philadelphia has been the location of several major ethnographic studies by Anderson, Goffman, and Lee.[6]

Table 5.2 shows a socio-demographic profile of the thirty-six Chinese immigrant entrepreneurs I interviewed. Most of them were in their early- or mid-forties and have been in the United States for about twenty years. More than 90 percent of them are married with the educational attainment of middle school or high school. Their work experiences show very striking patterns. For example, while 55 percent used to work in New York City, more than 40 percent skipped New York City and went directly to new destinations. This is quite different from following the traditional wisdom of concentrating settlement in gateway destinations such as New York City. Only about 10 percent of entrepreneurs had worked one job only. In fact, job histories showed that more than 60 percent had worked four or more jobs. Frequent job transition from employer to employer seems to be the new normal for this group of immigrant entrepreneurs. What is also revealing is that more than 40 percent of our interview subjects own two or more businesses. This new pattern of business ownership suggests that for many of these immigrant entrepreneurs, their American dream has moved away from the immigrant business model of survival to a model of real economic mobility.

DOING BUSINESS IN NEW IMMIGRANT DESTINATIONS

By now, the general pattern of spatial diffusion of immigrants in the United States has been firmly established. The larger story we learn from the experiences of Latino immigrants is that this pattern was mainly driven by industrial restructuring that opened up new employment opportunities for low-skilled immigrant workers in the service sector. As Massey summarizes, "industrial structuring creates an initial demand for immigrants in new locations and then processes of cumulative causation takes over to channel subsequent cohorts of migrants to these new destinations."[7] In new destinations, the restaurant industry benefits directly from this restructuring. In the Sun Belt, for example, population growth coupled with an increase in disposable income creates demand for restaurants and services. As native-born citizens (and high-skilled immigrants) move into these areas from other parts of the country, they also bring their taste for ethnic food with them.[8]

Results from our statistical models detailed in chapter 4 reveal some findings that are as we expected, namely that Chinese business owners tend to select places that are characterized by low unemployment rates, low crime, and middle income. However, unlike what the conventional wisdom would predict, Chinese business owners tend to select places with a low percentage of Asian and Chinese immigrants. This is also clear from examining table 5.1. The neighborhoods where we carried out interviews with business owners are home to only very tiny percentages of Asians or Chinese Americans. Despite the insights from these statistical models, we wanted to know more about the actual decision-making process guiding business in these locations, which will provide a complementary perspective compared to the work covered in chapter 4.

Chen is a restaurant owner in North Carolina who owns three restaurants there. He described the experience of buying the third restaurant: "I arrived in North Carolina in 1993, got a job in a Chinese restaurant. Over the years I have known a lot of local people. My landlord owns three properties all renting out for Chinese restaurant owners. When a Chinese restaurant owner decided to retire, the landlord asked me to consider buying that property. In fact, the landlord actually helped with getting the mortgage for the property.

So now I own the restaurant and the property as well thanks to the help of my landlord."

Another business owner in Corpus Christi, Texas, Mr. Zhang, has a similar experience. He arrived in the United States in 1994 and worked in Chinese restaurants in different states. In February 2010, his cousin, who owned a Chinese restaurant in Texas, saw an ad in a local newspaper for a property that he felt was perfect for a buffet-style Chinese restaurant. His cousin suggested that Mr. Zhang come to Texas to start his own business. His cousin said his restaurant was the only one in his neighborhood, which was a big advantage as there was no competition (*meiyou jingzheng*). Now he and his cousin are co-owners of this business and have invested $400,000 renovating it to help it grow. The majority of the customers are Mexican Americans, which is consistent with what we learn from table 5.1.

Like Mr. Zhang, almost all of the business owners we interviewed across six states began as workers in Chinese or Asian restaurants. This transition from worker to owner is actually consistent with the experiences of Jewish and Italian small business owners in New York City in the 1930s and 1940s.[9] Moreover, Bailey and Waldinger's argument about why this happened applies here as well. That is, Chinese immigrant-owned businesses work as a training system. As immigrants work in these businesses, they learn the skills and build necessary network connections which ultimately facilitate the launching of their own businesses in the future.

As mentioned earlier, two-fifths of immigrant entrepreneurs own more than one business. This finding also came out in our interviews with restaurant supply store owners in Manhattan. One business owner told me that "it is important to build a good relationship with restaurant business owners not only because they can recommend my service to their friends, but also some of them have multiple businesses that can all use my service."

One of the possible challenges of operating a business in places like Texas or Florida is a lack of Chinese immigrant workers in the local population. Employment agencies in Manhattan's Chinatown are one source of workers, but the restaurant owners we interviewed explained that they used other recruitment strategies as well. Overall, roughly 50 percent of business owners reported using employment agencies in New York City. The other 50 percent hired either relatives/associates or local residents in the new destinations. One owner in Texas stated: "Mexican and white workers tend to walk into the door to look for jobs. It is not easy to get a job around here, so they (local workers) like to work for me. We prefer not to hire workers introduced from employment agencies because some of them do not have legal documentation and these folks, they work very hard and are easy to manage."

A business owner in Virginia mentioned to us that he employs relatives and some Mexican workers introduced by employment agencies in NYC. There are other interesting paths toward employment though, such as the white college student in Charlotte, North Carolina who liked a local restaurant's Japanese food so much that he decided to take on a part-time job that enabled him to eat at the restaurant for free! Like any restaurant, there is also a hierarchy along the lines of workers' race and ethnic background.[10] In an ethnographic study of high-end restaurants in Los Angeles, Wilson found that most white workers work in the front end of the business, characterized by prestige, higher pay, and more interaction with customers. Conversely, Latino workers tend to work in the "back end of the business," busing tables, washing dishes, and cooking. Wilson finds that bilingual workers (who speak both English and Spanish) serve as brokers to smooth out relations between the two groups.

In Chinese immigrant-owned restaurants, there tend to be three types of workers: Chinese immigrants, Latinos (primarily from Mexico), and whites.[11] Chinese workers typically work as chefs, kitchen helpers, or cashiers. Latino/Mexican workers often work as busboys or dish washers, and white workers' typical jobs are servers and bartenders because they possess better language and communication skills.[12] It is often the case that Chinese workers get paid the highest salaries, followed by white workers, then Mexicans, who are at the bottom of pay scale. White workers get very good hourly wages, but their total pay is lower than that of the Chinese workers because employers usually only allow them to work part time (never exceeding forty hours a week). Walter is a Chinese immigrant who owns a Japanese restaurant. He said, "hiring a white worker, you have to watch out [for] the work hours, eight hours a day and forty hours a week. If a white worker exceeds forty hours a week, I have to pay twice the salary. But Chinese workers are more acceptable." By "acceptable," Walter means that it is totally acceptable that Chinese workers get the same pay rate for overtime work that they do for regular work.

In a study of Indian-owned motels in the United States, sociologist Pawan Dhingra informs us that Indian immigrant motel owners often place white employees at the front desk to create a "mainstream business impression" instead of looking like an immigrant-owned business.[13] Chinese business owners like Walter did something similar. He said that "hiring white workers is the demand from the market, not a requirement from me. As a Japanese restaurant, we mainly cater to middle class customers. If we hire white workers, it makes the restaurant look quite distinctive as compared to other Chinese restaurants with all Chinese workers." Walter also added that it is often a good idea to hire white women at the bar because most of the time people who drink at the bar are men who want to chat with women. "I also hire some white men for bartender job[s] because they know how to talk sports and hot news items. A good bartender can get you many return customers because they enjoy talking to the bartender."

Another entrepreneur is Mr. Yong Zheng, who owned several restaurants in North Carolina and sold them a couple of years ago. His brother still owns eight restaurants in South Carolina. Mr. Zheng hired many workers from different backgrounds over the years while his restaurant was in operation. Here is what he said:

> Frankly, I pay a little bit higher salary for white workers as compared to my Chinese workers. From my perspective, this is really worth it

because when white workers pick up the phone for food delivery, they make customers very comfortable and sometimes crack some small jokes here and there. I also hire white workers as bartenders, they know how to talk to local people. Ultimately this helps with my business. The local white employees are also very stable, and they stay on one job for a long time. I want job stability. Mexicans work hard, but they tend not to have a long-time perspective for their career. I really want to train Mexican workers and to move them to chef jobs, if they can promise to stay long. Unfortunately, for many Mexican workers, once they feel they make enough money, they can leave you. The Chinese workers leave you because you are not paying them enough (or he gets a better offer somewhere else). The Mexican workers leave you because they feel they have enough money.

ADAPTING TO NEW DESTINATIONS

From our interviews, it is clear that most of these owners have relatives and friends in New York City. So how do these immigrant entrepreneurs manage to adapt in new destinations? First, I note that most of these business owners are married and have children. Several of our informants mentioned the role of children in serving as cultural brokers to communicate with those outside the family. One owner in Ohio said, "I do not speak English well and lots of times I depend on my children. My children help with the restaurant business after school. They help with all the other businesses involved in English."

Our interviews showed evidence that the business owners were integrating into their new communities. In this regard, immigrant entrepreneurs who work in the restaurant business have some advantages because almost by definition, people who are in the restaurant business have to interact with local people, whether that be speaking on the phone, coordinating deliveries, or interfacing with customers. This means both sides have to make an effort to understand each other. As table 5.2 shows, most immigrant entrepreneurs do not possess much formal education, but many have worked hard to learn the new language and some of them are now very good at communication with customers. One successful example is a restaurant owner in Virginia. His restaurant walls are all decorated with photos he has taken with local people and celebrities. Among them are police officers, firefighters, soldiers, doctors, and lawyers. He is firmly entrenched in the local community and contributes to it regularly, such as through his frequent donations to local middle and high school sports programs. He is considered to be a model of success for immigrants in new destinations.

During our interviews, we also found that some of the second generation or 1.5 generation Chinese population are involved in the restaurant business, very often successfully.[14] Liu, who owns a restaurant in Key West, is one such example. Liu's father was a sailor who jumped ship in Los Angles in 1982. Luckily, as an agricultural worker at the time, his father was eligible for the amnesty program created by the 1986 Immigration Reform and Control Act and was able to receive a permanent resident (green) card. Liu's father applied for immigration visas for Liu and his mother and sister in 1989 when Liu was eight years old. That same year, Liu's father bought a restaurant from a man from Taiwan. Two years later, by the age of ten, Liu had learned English and was able to answer the phone in the restaurant after school. Meanwhile, his thirteen-year-old sister could communicate with customers and translate when health inspectors came to review the restaurant. From an early age, Liu learned the business from his parents.

In 2003, when Liu was about to get married, his father decided to give the restaurant to him as a wedding gift. Today, he very much enjoys running the restaurant and seeing all of the return customers who have come there for more than twenty years (counting the years when the restaurant was owned by the immigrant from Taiwan). Because he attended local elementary, middle, and high schools, he knows many of his customers as former classmates and teachers, all of whom have come to see Liu as just another part of their community. He has been invited to local parties, weddings, church gatherings, and funeral services for local friends. His integration into the community is evident in his relationship with a regular customer who lived alone. Her son, a well-known judge in Miami, would stop by the restaurant whenever he was in town to see his mom. He once told Liu's food delivery person that should he ever notice that the house lights were not on at night, he should call for help immediately so that someone could check on his mother. Indeed, there is certainly a lot of trust placed in Mr. Liu and his staff members by the community.

He has a very strong local identity. Because he came to the United States at the age of eight and belongs to the "1.5 generation," he has no nostalgia for his father's hometown in China. He also does not have a lot of connections with New York City, like other first-generation immigrants do. He does, however, go fishing with his friends (some are Chinese, others are not) every week. He said, "I like the blue sky, I enjoy fishing, we are here to enjoy life, not to make money." Clearly, this 1.5-generation business owner has a different philosophy on life compared to many first-generation immigrants.

One important sociological finding exemplified in this story is that some Chinese restaurants have been in operation for so long that they have become local institutions. They are part of local daily life and even help make up the "mainstream" culture in the community. In this regard, it is worth mentioning that all of the business owners we interviewed bought houses locally. This is true regardless of whether they do business in middle class neighborhoods or in low-income neighborhoods.

Church is another institution that helps immigrants integrate into the local community. One restaurant owner mentioned happily that he was often invited by local white customers to Thanksgiving and Christmas gatherings at local churches where he would make new social connections with other churchgoers. Certain new destinations even have churches that offer religious services in Chinese. Some of the business owners in Florida go to church every Sunday with a service in Chinese and attend Bible study session on Friday.

When asked, they claim that they do not feel lonely at all, indicating that church membership can lead to a richer, more fulfilling life for immigrants.

All of the business owners in our sample bought properties in these new destinations. Cleary, they have realized their version of the American dream. Some own many restaurants, with one of our interviewees having purchased as many as ten properties. This is a new pattern in the sense that they treat the restaurant business as a modern organization, such that when business is good, they expand. However, the economy has its ups and downs. One business owner in Florida bought four houses and one restaurant in 2001, only to eventually lose $300,000 of his investment when housing values plummeted during the global financial crisis in 2008.

RACE RELATIONS IN NEW DESTINATIONS

For sociologists who study immigrants in new destinations in the United States, perhaps one of the most important questions concerns the inter-group relations between local residents (often minority residents) and immigrants. This is a departure from typical studies of black and white relations that have dominated the field by looking at relationships between minority groups. Extant research is often based on the case of Latino immigrants in new destinations, which shows some level of accepting Latino immigrants. However, Fennelly's focus group study with local white residents in Minnesota reveals that some local residents are really concerned that newcomers may bring crime, economic competition, and an increased tax burden to their communities.[15] Marrow reports a more complicated portrait of race relations between Hispanics and African Americans in North Carolina.[16] In the economic arena, Marrow shows that a community with a high concentration of African Americans experiences a stronger sense of threat when new Hispanic immigrants arrive.[17] However, this level of threat is not felt strongly in the arena of local politics. Tropp et al. surveyed US-born groups (whites and blacks) and immigrant groups (Mexicans and Indians) in Atlanta and Philadelphia, revealing that a greater frequency of contact between groups leads to feelings of welcoming and being welcomed.[18] Telles et al. present a complex relationship between Latino immigrants and African Americans that often depends on sociodemographic factors as well as local communities and institutions.[19] We too anticipate some possible complex scenarios regarding race relations in neighborhoods based on the racial/ethnic makeup of local populations.

Before I continue my discussion of race relations in new destinations, it is important to have a sense of comparison between the context for race relations in New York City and in those new destinations.[20] I see at least three differences between the two contexts. First, because New York is quintessential a city of immigrants with its long history of receiving new arrivals from so many countries, local people are generally used to a social environment populated with other immigrants and immigrant business owners. That is not the case in many new immigrant destinations, however. Second, there are many immigrant hometown associations and Chinese churches in New York City that can provide advice for dealing with issues of race or strategies for addressing possible discrimination or other crises when they happen. Third, there are some business owners in New York City who do focus almost entirely on doing business with Chinese immigrant customers. For them, business interactions with others outside the Chinese immigrant community are limited. This is certainly not possible for immigrants in new destinations. To explore race relations, in our survey of restaurant owners in six states, we asked the following question: Do you perceive discrimination from local residents? All of our respondents answered no. We also asked: Do you say hi to local residents when you meet them? All respondents answered in the affirmative. So on the surface, things look good.

However, a deeper analysis of interview materials suggests a complex story. We have three kinds of neighborhoods based on the locations of the business owners we interviewed. The first is the kind of neighborhood with a majority of white residents, such as the neighborhood in Ohio. From our fieldwork, we note that people generally feel safe in these communities. We did not hear of any encounters that rise to the level of a major conflict. However, there were some reported unpleasant and unwelcome incidents experienced by business owners, especially during the global financial crisis of 2008 and soon after. In Dayton, Ohio, in the aftermath of the crisis, local workers (mostly blue-collar and white) were hit hard by the contracting economy and some lost their jobs. It is in this context that one restaurant owner shared the following story: "Very often you will have a white worker come in and order $15 worth of food and drink. When the meal and drink are ready, the person will grab them, leave only $10, and start running towards the door." The restaurant owner rationalized that the job market was tough and they were lucky to have some business anyway.

Another business owner complained about what he took to be intimidation by local white workers who perceive some of the Chinese immigrants as vulnerable. "I think they (local customers) were bullying Chinese people," he said. "On several occasions, after finishing their meals, some customers might say that the food did not taste good, the restaurant was unsanitary, and they wanted refunds. Otherwise, they will call police or ICE." This owner took the issue to the next level by saying, "the United States does not respect human rights. We are honest people and work hard, but can easily become the subject of bullying by local people." The same business owner also shared with us the following incident. One day in 2009, a white worker (perhaps unemployed at the time) came in and yelled at the staff, "Your Chinese people stole jobs from us and I am going to call ICE to arrest all of you!" The owner ended up giving him some free food and ushered him to the door, but the next day, several workers quit. This evidence of discrimination and intimidation reaffirms the notion that in times of economic crisis, immigrants are often the first to be blamed.

The second kind of neighborhood we studied is the Hispanic neighborhood in Texas. In Corpus Christi, restaurant owners all reported that business was good and that Mexican Americans seemed to love Chinese food. Some immigrant entrepreneurs who had worked in other states before settling in Texas went so far as to say that money was easy to make there. The only complaint they mentioned to us is that they wished the tips were more generous.

The third type of neighborhood is represented by the location with a majority of black residents in northern Philadelphia, where there has been a strong connection between African Americans and Chinese food. Reporter Louis Beck wrote in 1898 that black Americans were among the first fans of Chinese food.[21] Haiming Liu reports that there were several early chop suey houses in uptown Manhattan that catered mostly to African American customers.[22] Louis Armstrong, the famed African American jazz musician, wrote "Cornet Chop Suey" in 1926. According to Ricky Riccardi, Armstrong's love of Chinese food started during his childhood and lasted throughout the rest of his life.[23]

The story for owners in northern Philadelphia is sociologically more interesting and in fact can inform the literature on merchant-customer relations between immigrants and native-born minorities, especially blacks. When we analyzed zip code-level data for a basic socioeconomic profile of our neighborhood in northern Philadelphia, it revealed a very high percentage of blacks (nearly 60 percent), with a high proportion of local residents living below the poverty line. We also noted that black householders disproportionally work in physically demanding jobs with unpredictable hours, making take-out food more appealing in many instances. In this regard, it is similar to neighborhoods described by Weitzer, who studied race relations between Korean merchants and black residents in Washington, DC.[24] Not surprisingly, this is a rich sociological field in which several recent major ethnographic studies have been carried out. Anderson provides a penetrating and sharp analysis of poverty, drug culture, and interactions between blacks and whites in a similar neighborhood.[25] Lee studies this community from the perspective of merchant-customer relations (namely those between Korean entrepreneurs and black customers).[26] Goffman adds another ethnographic study of crime, incarceration, and injustice in the same neighborhood where we conducted interviews.[27]

Although these neighborhoods in northern Philadelphia may be poor, Chinese restaurant owners tell us that business is good because of the high demand for quick and inexpensive Chinese take-out food. With high unemployment rates and large families, black household members frequently opt for Chinese take-out. While regular middle-class families may go to a restaurant once a week, business owners say it is not unusual that black customers in this neighborhood will order food twice a day.

The setup of a typical Chinese take-out establishment here is very different from what we see in a middle-class neighborhood. In most cases, the take-out place is on the first floor of a two-story house. It is a small space with no customer seating. There is often an ATM machine, but also visible in the corner of the ceiling is surveillance equipment. The most surprising thing for the first-time visitor is that there are usually bullet-proof windows at the counter, like something you might see at a bank. The owners say that they leave the bullet-proof windows open during the day and only use them at night when things can be much less predictable. A quick Google search of "Chinese restaurants in Philadelphia" will take you to many photos and reports of robberies and murders of Chinese restaurant owners and delivery men. This shouldn't be so surprising, as Chinese business owners tell us they are used to hearing gunshots at night. After all, these are dangerous neighborhoods. Another surprising fact is that the restaurants remain open until 2:00 a.m. This is another indication that a substantial number of people are not on a nine to five work schedule. Rather, they simply order food any time of the day when they feel hungry.

Despite yielding good profits, doing business in this kind of neighborhood is by no means easy. First, this is a dangerous neighborhood and crime is an unfortunate and ever-present reality. Chen, who owns a take-out restaurant along with his wife, described what happened in 2018.

> We usually go to bed around 2:00 a.m. when the business has closed. One day, at about 3:00 a.m., I smelled some melting iron. Before I knew it, the second-floor door burst open. Two masked African American men yelled, 'Cash and gold!' I knew it was a robbery. My children were sleeping in the room close to the door where the robbers entered. One man grabbed my daughter as a hostage, knowing that I would do anything they ask for, as long as they control my kids. They grabbed some $2000–$3000 cash along with some jewelry and then left. Luckily none of us were hurt. We called 911. When the police came, they told us that the robbers had cut the iron gate [hence the smell] to the third floor before entering on the second floor. The long-term consequence of this crime was that my daughter (seven years old at that time) was really scared which resulted in some psychological problems that required professional help for the next year. After that, we installed an alarm system with the help of the Fujianese Immigration Hometown Association of Philadelphia.

Besides the real risk of crime, immigrant restaurant owners have to deal with other unpleasant situations. Some customers will come to order food, and then report that they are short a quarter or 50 cents, though owners will usually just let that go. In another case, a customer told the cashier that they paid with a $5 bill, but had in reality only given a $1 bill. In this situation, the owner then suggested that the police be called to help review the surveillance camera footage, only to have the customer say, "Let's not worry about it." Another thing that gives business owners headaches is teenagers that congregate after school in front of the restaurant without buying anything. When asked to leave, these teenagers often respond with foul language. This sort of behavior negatively affects the restaurant business. Ms. Song reported that her business is in a neighborhood marked by drug and alcohol problems. One time, she says, there was a black resident who walked into the takeout restaurant in the middle of the night and shouted at the restaurant workers using bad language. The next morning, when he came back, Ms. Song asked him if he remembered what he had done earlier. The man replied that he did not remember anything because he had drunk too much. He then apologized for his behavior the night before.

What is interesting to observe in this kind of neighborhood is that the owners and customers may sometimes have a tense relationship but things very rarely get out of control. Escalating developments, like the boycotting of immigrant-owned businesses that Min and Yoon have reported in studies of conflicts between blacks and Koreans,[28] have not happened in these neighborhoods in northern Philadelphia. On the surface, some level of civility is on display in this kind of neighborhood, with no large-scale conflicts between merchants and local residents.[29] In the west Philadelphia neighborhood that Lee studied, everybody seemed to do their share in maintaining this level of civility, merchants and local residents alike.[30] So what is the story here in Northern Philadelphia?

First, to reduce potential tension and conflict, business owners always have an immigrant woman at the "front end," since women are perceived to be friendlier and less confrontational. Immigrant women often speak better and clearer English than men as well, and tend to have better communication skills. Most of these businesses are run by husband-wife teams. In general, the wife will greet customers, take the order, and collect the money, while the husband prepares the food. Mr. Chen, whose business was once robbed, said, "I do not know any woman who works in the kitchen because this is very demanding work physically." In fact, this "front end of the business" strategy has long been used by Jewish and Korean merchants who operate businesses in black neighborhoods.[31] Jennifer Lee documented an incident in which a Korean woman went out to break up a fight between two black men in the store front.[32] When asked why the woman's husband did not go instead, the husband said, "What if they fight me instead, if I try to break up the fight?"

Second, some business owners also use religion as a means to reduce pressure and maintain a good mental state. Ms. Song said:

"This is high-pressure work and we work fourteen hours a day (12 noon to 2:00 a.m.). You can lose your temper easily in this kind of neighborhood." Ms. Song and her husband use religious messages to increase their tolerance threshold. When Ms. Song invited us inside the restaurant, we saw that they had posted two messages on the other side of the bulletproof windows. One message, written in Chinese characters, reads "tolerance" (*rennai*). Another message on the inside window is from the Bible: "Love is persistent patience and tolerance." Because these religious messages are posted on the inside of the bulletproof window, they can only be seen by the restaurant owners, not the customers. Thus, these messages help provide some relief and comfort for restaurant owners who sometimes have to deal with a tough work environment. It doesn't hurt that religion is also a bonding force between Chinese immigrants and black residents, given that many of the black residents are also Christians.

When immigrants operate businesses in black communities, one of the most effective ways to defuse tension is to hire local black residents. Korean merchants in western Philadelphia have done this[33] and Chinese restaurant owners follow the same strategy. Ms. Song said that she wanted to pay a local elderly black woman to help clean the areas in the front of the restaurant. The elderly woman does the work every day, but does not want to be paid. Ms. Song said the most important role this elderly woman plays is dealing with teenagers. When teenagers stay too long in front of the restaurant, the woman will ask them to go home, which is always more effective than when Ms. Song asks them herself. Chinese restaurants also have tried to build more ties to the local community by contributing food for community events.[34]

Immigrant business owners who have children sometimes find that the children can work wonders in easing race relations and facilitating communication, which ultimately makes the business more successful. Most studies in this area document children as cultural brokers who help immigrant families have access to healthcare providers, schools, and other community resources.[35] Likewise, in a tough social environment such as northern Philadelphia, children can also help parents navigate inter-group relations. Ms. Wang, who owns a takeout place with her husband, shared the following touching story:

> When my son John was born, we decided to send him back to China to be taken care of by his grandparents. When my husband and I started the business in this new neighborhood, we bought the two-story house and decided to take John back to live with us in this new environment. Being away from us for so long, John initially was not very close to us. To be on the safe side, we always told John that it is not safe to play outside in this kind of neighborhood. To our surprise, John did not perceive any danger here. He went to a nearby park to watch black kids playing basketball. When he came home, he said the black kids treated him nicely and were enjoying other kids watching them play ball. At that time, the pastor from church told me to spend more time with John. So I asked [my] niece (a high school student at the time) to watch my business so that I could accompany John to the local park. It was during my time in the park that I got to know a lot of my black customers. It was the first time that I had some contact with my customers outside of my business. I learned to have some regular conversations with them in the park and got to know them better. That lasted about a year, during which time I often had black customers stop by to say hi even if they did not buy anything. I really have a sense that they see me as their friend. My perception of local black people has changed.

Certainly, social contact with local residents promoted understanding of black people in the neighborhood.[36] Ms. Wang continued,

> John clearly feels very comfortable talking to black kids. In fact, once when we discussed safety and security issues, John told us that black kids did bad things sometimes because they do not have a mother and father at home. I asked him, how do you know that? He said, whenever it got dark no one asked them to go home. Sometimes, it looks like their grandmas ask them to go home. . . . One day John returned home and said that a black kid was hungry and he wanted to bring some chicken wings to him. Worried about whether John might be

bullied by black kids to force him to bring food from the restaurant, I said everything in the restaurant needs to be paid for. If you help me clean some of the seafood, you can bring chicken wings to your friend. Guess what? John really spent one hour doing that. When he brought fried chicken wings to his black friend though, he had already left. That made John very sad and I regretted what I did. From that point on, whenever he said he wanted to go to the park and bring food with him, I always said ok, knowing full well that John was going to share the food with his black friends.

As we can see, as a teenager, John already realized that the other kids in his neighborhood were largely from non-traditional families, a well-established finding for sociologists. John's willingness to be engaged in the local community actually helps his parents' business. Ms. Wang shared the following stories with us: "When John was in high school, every day around 3 or 4 o'clock, there was always a group of kids that would come over to buy some snacks and hang out in the restaurant for a long time. Whenever this happened, I asked John to talk to them. It looks like John is their boss, because they all left after John would talk to them. What really makes John something of a hero is when he decided to join the army after high school. Several black military training officers came to my house to express their appreciation for John's decision to serve the country." This story calls back to a mass school shooting in Florida in 2018 where another son of a Fujianese restaurant owner, Peter Wang (no relation), was fatally shot while holding the door as other students fled. Peter also wanted to join the army and his dream was to attend the United States Military Academy at West Point. Peter was later admitted to the class of 2025 posthumously.[37] Ms. Wang continued her story:

> Since John joined the army, I often have visitors from the local Veterans Association. They always say that if there is anything I need, just to let them know. Specifically, if anyone starts to cause trouble for our business, they will take care of them. In the summer of 2020, at the height of the Black Lives Matter (BLM) movement, they called us

several times and advised us to close the business and hide somewhere for safety. They said the looters are not local people. My restaurant was damaged, but the next day, to my pleasant surprise, local
black neighbors came to my restaurant to clean the broken glass and
remove the graffiti done by the looters. I was truly moved by that.

In this case, social integration with the local community through
John's cultural brokerage led to local people's acceptance of newcomers as members of their community. When the newcomers experienced trouble, local residents and organizations (like the Veterans
Association) came to the rescue.

John's story has another happy ending. One of the major challenges expressed by Chinese business owners in this neighborhood
is their children's education. Some parents send their children to
a bilingual institution in Chinatown that is only available through
elementary school. For middle school and high school, there are two
options. One is to take a test to potentially go to one of the elite private schools in Philadelphia, and the other is to attend one of the
local public schools, which are not known to be of high quality. John
has a younger brother, Jason, who his parents wanted to see attend
a local Catholic school. The selection process involves two routes.
For 50 percent of the students, parents pay regular tuition (about
$30,000 a year). The rest of the 50 percent are selected by lottery.
Ms. Wang tried the lottery but was not successful. Just when the
parents were about to give up, a local black church leader came to
the restaurant and learned about this. He said that he was going
to talk to the Catholic school, because now that John was in the
army, he could not take care of his little brother. Soon afterward, the
school informed Ms. Wang that another student had decided not to
come and a position was now open. Happily, Jason got the chance to
attend the Catholic school.

Before I finished interviewing Ms. Wang, I asked her if there was
a light-hearted moment that she could share about doing business
in this tough environment. She paused for a moment and replied
while smiling: "Yes, sometimes customers come in and say 'ni hao'

[hello]. That brightens my heart. One day, an African American lady walked in and asked me, 'How to say you are crazy in Chinese?' I told her '*shen jingbing*.' She cheerfully said, 'next time you see me, just call me '*shen jingbing*'.' A conversation like this goes a long way to smoothen relationships between immigrants and local residents.

FROM INDIVIDUAL RESPONSES TO COLLECTIVE ACTION

Given the high crime rate in these neighborhoods in northern Philadelphia,[38] the biggest concern among Chinese immigrant business owners is robbery. The Fujianese Association of Greater Philadelphia has sponsored workshops for business owners on crime prevention and safety. The Association has also been in constant contact with the local police department to make sure that when disturbances around Chinese businesses occur, police will arrive on a timely basis. In addition, Chinese business owners donate money to sponsor Community Policing in their neighborhoods.

Violence against Chinese business owners and employees has been going on for a while. The robberies and murders of Chinese business owners are frequently reported.[39] In 2014, rapper YG posted a video on YouTube entitled "Meet the Flockers," which openly encourages people to rob Chinese-owned businesses and homes. The lyrics began with the following: "First you find a house and scope it out. Find a Chinese neighborhood 'cause they don't believe in bank accounts." The Chinese community and business leaders were outraged but YG and his supporters cited freedom of expression in his defense.

The year 2016 was an important moment for anti-violence collective action by the Chinese community in Philadelphia. In that year, a record number of violent crimes took place against Chinese business owners. In the month of January alone, twelve such crimes were reported. YG was planning on giving a concert on October 15, 2016, so in response, Chinese community leaders chose October 15

Figure 5.2. Anti-violence rally in Philadelphia, October 15, 2016.

for a big rally against violence. More than two thousand Chinese immigrants from Philadelphia, New York City, and Delaware joined the rally along with representatives from the Philadelphia Police Department, the American Civil Liberties Union, the Chinese Immigrant Associations in New York and Philadelphia, and local church leaders. Also making history was the fact that members from the Chinese Rifle Association in the Greater Philadelphia area (CRAGP) carried rifles during the parade (see figure 5.2). The participation of CRAGP was intended to send a message to perpetrators that Chinese immigrants are not always an easy target for crime, but can defend their rights with weapons as well.[40]

FURTHER REFLECTIONS

In the sociological literature, two models characterize the relationship between immigrant business owners and local black residents. One is a model of conflict and confrontation, as depicted by mass media and scholars like Min and Yoon.[41] The second is a model of civility, whereby all parties (immigrant business owners, their employees, and local blacks) "make considerable investment in maintaining civility under conditions of extreme inequality."[42] Our survey found that the experiences of Chinese immigrant business owners in Northern Philadelphia are probably somewhere in between: even in an extremely dangerous business environment, they manage to maintain a reasonable level of civility and avoid open confrontation with minority group members. However, Chinese immigrant entrepreneurs do sponsor protests and rallies to promote awareness of crimes and violence against Chinese businesses. This has the effect of educating law enforcement officers who can then better protect Chinese business interests down the road.

The logic of Chinese immigrant entrepreneurs' approach to race relations can be elaborated on in the following way. First, at the most basic level, immigrant owners are convinced that only by maintaining good relationships with local black people can their businesses survive and provide a way of making a living. During interviews, entrepreneurs always mentioned to us how much they appreciated the opportunity to do business in these kinds of communities. Some went as far as to say, "Our parents gave us life but African Americans give us economic opportunities." Their deep appreciation of African American customers is on full display. Compared to white-dominated middle-class neighborhoods, business in black neighborhoods is very stable, with little fluctuation, and operating costs are lower. One business owner said that a similar commercial property (such as his two-story building) in a middle-class white neighborhood would cost at least $160,000 more.

Second, most of these small business owners live and work in the same building. This is different from the model of Korean business owners in black communities, who more often work in the black community but reside outside of it. For Chinese immigrants in northern Philadelphia, it is in their best interest to maintain good relationships with local residents because they are in those communities twenty-four hours a day. An important message from the story of Ms. Wang (the business owner whose son joined the army) is that social integration through children's cultural brokerage protects business interests in the community. At this point, though, there are still immigrant business owners in black neighborhoods who are afraid to let their children play outside. Third, also unlike the case of Korean merchants, a sizable number of Chinese business owners still do not have legal immigration status. As such, they are afraid of any publicity should any conflict or confrontation with local black residents lead to some kind of media coverage which might get them into trouble with immigration enforcement officers. However, this third factor is becoming less important over time as many business owners are able to receive green cards.

6 The Ties That Bind

BETWEEN CHINATOWN IN MANHATTAN
AND NEW IMMIGRANT DESTINATIONS

For more than a century, Chinatowns in the United States have been a place for many Chinese immigrants to settle and work. They have provided a comfortable and familiar environment. Here, immigrants can work for Chinese employers, eat Chinese food, and speak their native language/dialect. For some Chinese immigrants, Chinatowns simply provide a first point of entry into the job market in the United States. When another opportunity arises, they move on, though they may come back to Chinatown at some other point as a tourist or visitor, perhaps during vacation or on a business trip to New York City. Others choose to stay in Chinatown permanently. From a labor market perspective, Chinatown has been a "job machine" for many generations of Chinese immigrants. Today, Chinatown is still more or less a job machine even for those who do not stay locally; it is a launching point for immigrants who come to Chinatown to get job information and then get on one of the Chinatown buses to pursue work in another location in the country.

Two questions motivate this chapter. First, once immigrant entrepreneurs and workers move away from New York City, do they maintain connections with Chinatown? And if so, in what ways? Spatial settlement patterns have been at the forefront of recent immigration research. Much of this literature views settlement patterns as part of a spatial assimilation process.[1] The idea is that when immigrants first arrive in the United States, they tend to settle in or close to immigrant neighborhoods or ethnic enclaves such as Chinatown. As immigrants improve their English language skills and gain more experience in the job market, they tend to assimilate in terms of their settlement patterns, namely moving into mainstream middle-class neighborhoods with good school districts and better amenities.[2]

However, this conventional conceptualization of immigrant settlement patterns (also knowns as the spatial assimilation model) tends to focus only on a particular city or metropolitan area.[3] Previous researchers did not quite anticipate the large number of migrants who would move to another location altogether, instead of settling in suburban neighborhoods. Geographer Wei Li's work did note a new pattern for immigrants who move to "ethno-burb" areas, suburban environments with a diverse group of immigrants from several countries.[4] Flippen and Farrell-Bryan provide the most updated review in the literature on new immigrant destinations, focusing on three major dimensions.[5] First, this literature pays major attention to new segregation patterns of immigrants in new and traditional destinations, rather than to the long tradition of studying immigrant adaptation and assimilation. Second, this body of literature also examines new destinations and status attainment, which includes education, labor market outcomes, home ownership, and health outcomes. Finally, this literature also deals with the extent to which long-term residents respond to the arrival of immigrants in new destinations. Although current literature has covered numerous dimensions of outcome variables in new destinations, researchers have not explored possible linkages between traditional and new destinations. Flippen and Farrell-Bryan call for more efforts to identify mechanisms related to outcomes of immigrants in new destinations.

What is often missing in the current literature on new immigrant destinations is a discussion of how links are created and maintained between traditional gateway destinations and new destinations. Understanding these linkages can also help us gain insights into possible outcomes of immigrants in those new destinations. I see this line of inquiry as related to two lines of migration research. The first is the well-known and rising importance of transnationalism.[6] The rising popularity of this approach is aided by the current ease of international travel as well as communication technology that allows immigrants to maintain constant contact between people in countries of origin and countries of destination.[7] Levitt documents transnational linkages between the Dominican immigrant community in the United States and the immigrant-sending community back in the Dominican Republic. She focuses on economic, political, and religious linkages.[8]

A second line of relevant research is the translocal perspective (or translocalism). Lohnert and Steinbrink have developed the translocal perspective to capture the interdependence between rural and urban locations in the context of South Africa.[9] This concept captures the lives of an increasingly important segment of rural households that are dependent on both locations. In my earlier work on rural-urban migration in China, I used this framework to examine migrant entrepreneurs who take advantage of China's transportation infrastructure in order to pursue a new form of migrant translocal entrepreneurship.[10] Although we can see parallels with both transnationalism and translocalism, I think that since translocalism deals with immigrants/migrants in a country, it is more appropriate to conceptualize the Chinese immigrant entrepreneurs who are doing business in new US destinations as *translocal immigrant entrepreneurs*. This is a concept that aims to describe those Chinese immigrant entrepreneurs who move away from New York City, but

THE TIES THAT BIND 115

also continue to maintain different kinds of ties with Chinatown in Manhattan. It also applies to immigrants who work in new destinations as well. As I demonstrated in chapters 2 and 3, these translocal linkages are clearly shown when employers rely on employment agencies for workers who then use Chinatown buses to travel to new immigrant destinations. Beyond Chinatown buses and EAs, we also find that translocal immigrant entrepreneurs rely on a whole supply chain industry in Chinatown that provides essential services for the operation of Chinese restaurants across the United States. The quick rise of e-commerce in recent years only further facilitates this reliance on Chinatown's supply chain.

In this chapter, I pay particular attention to three aspects of cross-region/cross-local linkages: the economic, social, and religious connections between migrant origins and destinations. Our survey of immigrant entrepreneurs, discussed in the previous chapters, asked how much of a connection they maintain with Chinatown and with New York City in general. These interview materials show that these linkages are clearly manifested in the economic, social, and religious dimensions.

THE ECONOMIC TIES BETWEEN NEW YORK AND NEW DESTINATIONS

Initially, when we asked our respondents how many connections they maintain with New York City in terms of running their businesses and maintaining their social network, they often replied, "not much." When we probed further and let them reflect more, we found considerable evidence that these immigrant entrepreneurs continue to maintain strong ties with the Chinese immigrant and business community in New York City. In chapters 2 and 3, we have already glimpsed this reliance on services provided by people in Chinatown in Manhattan. In this chapter, I will focus more on a new set of players in Chinatown. No matter where their businesses are located, from Philadelphia to Florida, from Ohio to Texas, all of these immigrant entrepreneurs rely on Chinatown for ordering restaurant menus, buying cookware (such as pans, rice cookers, pots, dishes), cash registers, and surveillance equipment. In fact, Chinatown in New York City is the epicenter of anything related to Chinese restaurant operations in the United States.

Figure 6.1 shows the spatial distribution of shops related to the restaurant business in Chinatown. The locations of these shops also bear some unique spatial characteristics. One observation is that these shops are not located along Canal Street, which attracts a lot more tourists eating Chinese food and shopping for souvenirs. All of these restaurant supply shops are located in the vicinity of East Broadway, where the population of Fujianese immigrants dominates. Another observation is that there is a major concentration of these shops on both sides of Allen Street. They are encompassed by a triangular boundary formed by three streets: the Bowery on the west, Delancey on the northeast, and East Broadway on the south. The large concentration of printing shops that produce Chinese restaurant menus is found on Madison Street, two blocks from East Broadway. These printing shops are typically not very big. They often have large windows displaying different Chinese menu designs. All of these menus have clear addresses written on them; almost all of the restaurants are located outside of New York City, in places such as Indiana, North Carolina, Ohio, even Hawaii. Most of the menus are for Chinese restaurants, but these printing shops increasingly sell to Japanese restaurants as well.[11]

To learn more about the Chinatown shops that print restaurant menus, I interviewed Ms. Lynn Zheng, who owns a printing shop on Madison Street in Chinatown. A longtime business owner friend of mine owns a small seafood retail shop in Chinatown. Whenever I go to Chinatown, my first stop is always this shop. One day in the summer of 2017, when I mentioned interviewing some printing shop owners, my friend immediately thought of Ms. Lynn Zheng, because her business was located right around the corner. It turned out that

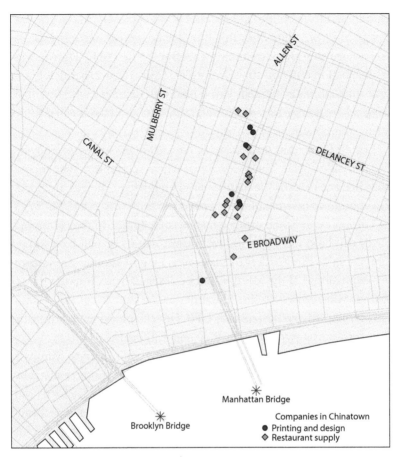

Figure 6.1. Spatial distribution of printing companies and restaurant supply shops in Manhattan's Chinatown.

Lynn was the daughter of another well-known Chinese immigrant entrepreneur who owned several restaurants and who was also active in the Chinese community before passing away a few years ago. I had known Lynn's father since I first did my survey of Chinese immigrants in Chinatown in the early 2000s.[12] Lynn said that her printing business was more or less envisioned by her father, who advised her to major in graphic design in college. Lynn added, "Not until

I graduated from college did I realize why I was majoring in graphic design." In 1997, soon after this, she started her business. It was the second printing shop in Chinatown, after the first one, "Hanyi," was established in 1995 on the same street. Lynn's father, being a long-time entrepreneur himself, was a business visionary who saw that demand would rise as many immigrant entrepreneurs opened more businesses outside of New York City.

Lynn told me that 90 percent of her customers are entrepreneurs from outside of New York (*waizhou*). When a restaurant owner contacts her, she designs the menus based on the food choices provided. The minimum number of menus per order is five thousand, but most restaurant owners will order ten thousand. Typically, four shipping boxes will hold ten thousand restaurant menus. When I asked her how she ships these orders to customers, I found another Chinatown bus connection! If the location can be reached by a Chinatown bus, the bus will be used to ship the order at the expense of the restaurant owner. Otherwise, she uses UPS. Her customers are all over the country, as far away as Puerto Rico and California.

One burning question for me is why customers turn to Manhattan's Chinatown when they could use other locations, especially customers whose businesses are closer to California. It turns out that the overwhelming majority of customers are from Fujian province and have a strong sense of connection and identity with Chinese immigrant businesses in Manhattan. When many immigrant business owners rely on Chinatown for business supplies such as menus, business volume increases, which allows people like Lynn to lower prices to gain a competitive edge. Perhaps this is the "Matthew effect" in the Chinese immigrant business community, a term referring to the cumulative advantage of economic capital. In other words, individuals become more successful because of earlier success.[13]

During our conversation, Lynn answered a couple of phone calls from customers. Sometimes she speaks in the Fuzhou dialect and sometime switches to Cantonese. I asked her about this and Lynn

Figure 6.2. Lynn's office at her printing company in Chinatown. Photo by Zai Liang.

said that she had spent some time in Hong Kong (where Cantonese is spoken) before coming to the United States.

Looking through hundreds of menus posted on the office walls (see figure 6.2), one can also learn something about the people who work in these restaurant-related businesses. For example, Lynn spoke of one time when she saw a menu for a restaurant in Washington, DC, that posted open hours until 3:00 a.m. She can also detect some new trends in the restaurant business earlier than others, such as the move toward Asian fusion food that combines Chinese, Thai, and Japanese. This is made clear by the fact that more Japanese restaurant menus are being printed in recent years. This observation is consistent with my interviews with people who are familiar with the restaurant business.

The second big business that immigrant entrepreneurs who work in other locations rely on is suppliers for the restaurant business. These stores are concentrated along Allen Street, just a short walk from East Broadway, which is the center of the Fujianese community

Figure 6.3. The biggest cookware shop in Chinatown. Photo by Zai Liang.

in Chinatown (figure 6.1). One sees primarily two kinds of businesses: those providing restaurant supplies and Chinatown bus companies. Stores related to the restaurant business sell cooking stoves, all sizes of rice cookers, cash registers, and surveillance camera systems. Essentially, all the equipment that you can imagine being necessary for restaurant operation can be purchased right in Chinatown. Figure 6.3 is a photo taken in the biggest cookware store in Chinatown. The store displays one of the largest selections of cookware that I have ever seen in my entire life!

Here, I want to share stories of two immigrant entrepreneurs who have been in the restaurant supply business for quite a while. Tim Chen operates a restaurant supply business on Pike Street in Chinatown. Tim is from Fujian province and is in his late fifties. He worked in Hong Kong for four years before coming to the United States in 1992. He worked for a few years in a restaurant in Harlem.

In 1996, he got started in the restaurant cookware supply business. Initially, he rented a small counter in a shop where he could run his business. Soon, he saw that business was booming and decided to expand. To do so, he needed to rent a larger space. The 1990s was a period of neighborhood transition, from a Cantonese speaking neighborhood to the one dominated by immigrants from Fujian province that we see today. The landlord is a Cantonese-speaking immigrant who had some misgivings about renting the space to an immigrant from Fujian. To convince the landlord, Tim said, "Look, even a person's five fingers have different lengths. Immigrants from Fujian are also different. For example, I am a Christian and you can really trust me." Finally, the landlord was persuaded. Soon he found himself needing to expand the business again, to its current location on Pike Street.

Tim's main business strategy is that when a new restaurant opens, he wants the business owner to order all of the things that the business needs from his shop. The main advantage is that he can then ship everything that has been ordered in one truck. Tim owns a big truck, which indicates he has constant demand for shipping that needs to be met. Tim also knows different business needs for restaurants in different kinds of neighborhoods. If a business is located in a mixed neighborhood (with a large concentration of African Americans and Latinos), there will be a higher demand for fried food, thus a higher demand for frying pans.

Tim is one of the most dedicated Christians among all of the entrepreneurs I talked to. He believes that "You have to love them (customers) before they love you." He applies these ideas to his business operation as well and tries hard to build good relationships with customers. Tim also told me that he had noticed a new pattern: his business outside of New York state is declining due to the shortage of restaurant workers lately. Right now, about half of his customers are located in New York City, with the other half around the country.

Next is the story of Mr. James Li, an immigrant from Fujian who owns a cookware store on Allen Street. James is in his mid-forties.

His uncle started this line of business in 1999 at a time when Chinese buffet restaurants were booming. Initially, James came to work with his uncle. While on the job, James learned the ins and out of this business. By 2002, James was confident enough to start his own company. About 70 to 80 percent of his customers come from outside of New York state. James said the key to success in his business is constantly adapting to a changing market. This means that when Chinese buffet restaurants are popular, you stock the cookware supplies to meet this demand. In recent years, many Chinese immigrant entrepreneurs have gotten into the Japanese restaurant market and James quickly adapted. Even the name of his company has two Chinese characters that mean Chinese and Japanese food.

His customers come from nearly every state in the United States, some as far away as Oregon and California. I wondered why a customer in Oregon would order cookware from a company in New York's Chinatown. James responded, "Restaurants need to have special kinds of appliances that one cannot find in regular stores. Because of our business volume is so high, we are able to negotiate a good price that will benefit all customers. In fact, even including shipping costs of $2000 to Chicago (for a full truck) and $4000–$5000 to California, we still end up ahead. Some of the appliances ship directly from China to California, which would be even cheaper for business clients in California." James also mentioned social networks. "Once a customer is happy with you, he will contact you when opening a new restaurant or upgrading their current restaurant setup. I have many return customers (*huitou ke*). Some big entrepreneurs even open ten or twenty restaurants, which generates a lot of business for me." In addition, he said he continually learns new things and new designs, to stay on top of the field. He often helps customers design the layout of a restaurant, a service that lots of customers appreciate. That too brings more business. The last time I talked to James was in the summer of 2020 when the country was still in the middle of the Covid-19 pandemic. I asked him how his business was going. "It is booming!" James replied. He sent me photos of his staff busy moving appliances in his warehouse in Brooklyn. I was at first surprised. Who would want to do business in the middle of this pandemic? It turned out that manufacturers were offering deep discounts because of overall slow business, which provided a good opportunity to buy appliances that restaurant owners might need in the future.

Tim's and James' businesses are telling examples of the economic linkages between immigrant entrepreneurs in new destinations and Manhattan's Chinatown. A large portion of their business comes from customers outside of New York. These stories of economic connections can be corroborated by immigrant entrepreneurs outside of New York state. Given the recent popularity of Japanese restaurants in the United States, which drives many Chinese immigrant entrepreneurs into the Japanese restaurant business, we also see some stores that sell plates and cookware for Japanese food. Zhang is an immigrant restaurant owner who went to a Texas town in 2006 and started his own business there in 2008. When he first opened his restaurant, he ordered kitchen equipment and plates from New York City. He even used a construction company from New York to renovate the restaurant, although he also hired local people to make sure the restaurant was in compliance with local fire and electricity requirements. In addition, others maintain economic ties in terms of using services provided by Chinatown. Chen, a business owner in Ohio, mentioned that he still uses an accountant in New York to fill out tax return forms each year because he started using the accountant when he was in New York City and feels very satisfied with the service.

Another major economic tie between immigrant business owners and Chinatown is the use of employment agencies (EAs) in New York City for hiring workers.[14] If a restaurant location is in New York, hiring workers is often not that difficult as there are many Chinese immigrant workers who need jobs. However, in faraway places such as Ohio and Texas, finding a Chinese immigrant worker is not an easy task. As discussed in earlier chapters, the emergence of EAs is a response to immigrant entrepreneurs' need to hire workers for jobs far away from traditional immigrant locations. Mr. Huang, who runs a business in Ohio, shared with us that "For skilled jobs we use EAs in NYC to hire workers, but for other jobs such as busboys, we just hire Mexican immigrant workers. In fact, we regularly place job ads for busboys in the front door of our business." Huang's restaurant has a total of fifteen employees. There are eleven Chinese immigrant employees (seven from Fujian province and four from other provinces). All Chinese immigrants were hired through EAs. There are also two Mexican immigrants and two white Americans who have been hired locally. Mr. Zhang, the restaurant entrepreneur in Texas, has a total of thirteen employees, five Chinese, five Mexicans, and three whites. He has hired Chinese and Mexicans through EAs and white workers locally. With the business in Texas, Mr. Zhang said sometimes he uses the service of an EA in Los Angeles. Another business owner in Texas (Wendy) mentioned: "We employ three Mexicans, three white workers, one worker from Singapore, and one from India. The local job market is not that good, so the Mexican and white workers just knocked at the door looking for jobs." For Chinese workers, Wendy and her husband use EAs in New York because although some of the Chinese immigrants do not have papers, they work hard and do not complain. Another business owner in North Carolina has hired six workers: two Mexicans, three white workers, and one Chinese immigrant. Again, the Mexicans and white workers just happened to come to the restaurant to look for work, whereas the Chinese workers were hired through an EA in New York.

The Chinatown bus is another way to link New York City with Chinese immigrants in faraway locations. Whenever Chinese immigrant entrepreneurs and workers travel to New York City, they rely on Chinatown bus company services as long as there is a nearby Chinatown bus stop. The biggest advantage to using Chinatown buses that is often reported by immigrant entrepreneurs is that they can speak Chinese to the bus operators. The Chinatown bus always stops in Manhattan's Chinatown, which is a location they often want to go to as well.[15]

THE SOCIAL CONNECTIONS BETWEEN NEW YORK
AND NEW IMMIGRANT DESTINATIONS

Migration often means moving away from migrants' typical social circles in their places of origin. Today in the age of new communication technology, and especially social media, one can still maintain connections with one's circles of friends and relatives. I want to examine how immigrant entrepreneurs' social circles have been maintained or redefined once they settle in new destinations. In our interviews with thirty-six immigrant entrepreneurs, we asked three questions regarding social ties between New York City and new immigrant destinations. The first question is, "How often do you go to NYC?" The second question is, "Do you attend any social events (weddings, children's birthday parties. . . .) in NYC?" The third question asks if immigrants return to New York when their friends or relatives encounter emergency situations. There is no doubt that most immigrants have some social connections (friends or relatives) in New York City and several of them say that their best friends are there.

Only two respondents said that they did not go to New York during the year prior to our survey. Most travel to the city several times a year. One respondent mentioned going ten times in one year to a certain doctor in New York. In fact, many immigrants find that it is not convenient to see doctors in their new business locations because of challenges with communicating medical terms in English. Mr. Zhang, who owns restaurants in Texas, actually left two of his children with his parents in New York when he moved, so he visits almost monthly. In fact, our fieldwork in Brooklyn (where the largest Fujianese immigrant neighborhood is now located) reveals that there is a growing concern among immigrant organizations and school teachers in New York that too many Fujianese parents leave their children in Brooklyn when they go off to work in another part of the country.

It should be noted that immigrant entrepreneurs are typically married and often co-own their businesses with their spouses. Thus, we do not observe spouse separation in our sample of business owners. However, for immigrant workers, the story is very different. Consider the case of Jonathan and his wife, who initially owned a business in Virginia but were forced to close in 2016 due to fierce competition. With a child under three and another on the way, Jonathan spent $2000 per month to rent an apartment for his family on 8th Avenue in Brooklyn while he worked in Deptford, New Jersey, about a hundred miles away. In 2017, when their second child was two years old, they decided to send the two kids back to China to be taken care of by the children's grandparents. The couple went to work in a restaurant in Indiana for two years, where the restaurant owner had rented a four-bedroom apartment nearby and allowed the couple to stay in one of the bedrooms. In 2019, fearing that starting another business in a new place would be too difficult, the couple bought a three-bedroom house in Brooklyn. Jonathan and his wife missed their children very much, so they ended up bringing them back to the United States. The timing worked out well though, because the oldest child was almost ready to begin attending school. Now his wife and the two kids live in one of the bedrooms in their 8th Avenue house in Brooklyn and they rent out the two other rooms for about $2000 per month, which helps pay the mortgage.

Jonathan's wife really enjoys living among Brooklyn's Fujianese immigrant community, where everything is convenient and safe. Their oldest child attends public school during the week and also goes to a Chinese language school on the weekends. They have easy access to doctors and any other amenities that they may need. Social support is readily provided by a network of other wives whose husbands work outside of New York. Jonathan happily shared with us, "Every day at 3 p.m., I use We-Chat to see my son when he gets home from school. Often the kids also show me their homework and art projects over We-Chat. Sometimes I feel guilty because my oldest child wants me to watch him play sports at school and I cannot join him." He added, "Fortunately, my boss is very accommodating and sometimes allows me to take different days off to attend special school events with my kids. I want to stay together with my family, but it is hard because the mortgage is $4,500 a month. I am not sure if we can afford that without taking in boarders." From time to time, Jonathan's boss is also nice enough to drive him to Chinatown in Philadelphia, from which he can easily travel to 8th Avenue in Brooklyn to see his family via Chinatown bus. Jonathan's story is representative of many restaurant workers who are separated from their families while working in restaurants across the country. In some sense, many immigrants anchor their families in the neighborhood of Brooklyn's 8th Avenue, even when they themselves cannot afford to live at home full time.

As for the question about attending social events (weddings, birthday parties etc.), most answer they do not go, but definitely give money on these occasions. Some respondents mentioned that they did attend many weddings of their middle school classmates and other friends. The same thing can be said about handling emergency situations with friends and relatives in New York.

FROM CONFERENCE CALLS TO SOCIAL MEDIA GROUPS: PRACTICING RELIGION IN NEW DESTINATIONS

In 2006, New York Times reporter Michael Lou described how Fujianese immigrant workers in new immigrant destinations were practicing a new form of religious service by calling in to a pastor's phone in New York City.[16] At that time, there were as many as one hundred immigrant workers participating in these phone calls with Pastor Chen from The Church of Grace to Fujianese. Chen Yingjie, an immigrant worker in Dowagiac, Michigan, said "Every time I call in, I know the Lord is alive, and there are brothers and sisters by my side."[17] This conference call service is provided by a church on Allen Street in Chinatown that mainly serves Fujianese immigrants. In the early 2000s when I did my survey of Fujianese immigrants in New York City, we actually used the basement of the church to conduct some interviews. For many Fujianese immigrants, when they first arrived in New York City, the Church of Grace to Fujianese facilitated their settlement. Today this church has branches in Brooklyn, Queens, New Jersey, and Philadelphia.

The role of religion in the adaptation of immigrants in the United States has long been a topic of sociological research.[18] Hirschman synthesizes the role of religion in three Rs: refuge, respect, and resources.[19] The first refers to the fact that a church or mosque can serve as a source of comfort and protection. The second refers to a way in which religion provides opportunities for status and a sense of self-worth. This is especially important as some immigrants may have experienced a downward social trajectory in the United States. The third refers to the experiences of many that religion provides a way to help immigrants assimilate in American society by providing more access to job connections and housing choices, among other things.

Fujianese immigrants are a particularly religious group. Many immigrants from Fujian have had prior exposure to Christianity back in their hometowns, as Fujian is among the earliest provinces in China to encounter Christianity.[20] Others were converted to the Christian faith once in the United States. One of the major challenges among immigrant workers/entrepreneurs who settle in new destinations is how to maintain their religious practices. This is important as students of immigrants have long recognized the importance of religion and church in the adaptation process of immigrants. In traditional destinations such as New York, many churches offer services in the native languages of immigrants. For example, there are a total of twenty-six Christian churches (twenty-three Protestant and three Catholic) in Manhattan that offer service in Mandarin, Cantonese, or the Fuzhou dialect. However, it is often the case that no such religious service is offered in immigrants' native language in new immigrant destinations.

Thus, in the mid-2000s, Pastor Chen from the Church of Grace began to preside over conference calls for Bible study, which he designed for immigrant workers in new destinations. One of the things Lou's article reveals is that these conference calls often commence late at night (such as 11:00 p.m.) because by this time, immigrant workers have finished their work for the day.[21] Because they take place at nighttime, it was decided that four pastors should rotate participating in these conference calls. However, in the last few years, things have changed. Social media has become a new vehicle for religious practice among immigrants in new destinations. After interviewing pastors in the Church of Grace to Fujianese in New York City and the same church in Philadelphia, we found that in both places, We-Chat groups for Bible study are the new normal, having replaced conference calls. We-Chat is a free social media service provided by the China-based Tencent Company and has more than 1 billion users around the globe. The benefits are clear. We-Chat is free and flexible. Anyone can start a We-Chat group and members can send questions and make comments at any time. Participants have the option to communicate through either voice or video conferences using We-Chat.

So, in this time of the rising popularity of social media, to what extent are religious linkages between New York City and new immigrant destinations maintained or modified? To learn more about this, we talked to Bernard Zheng, one of the leaders of the Church of Grace to the Fujianese in Manhattan. Very tall and soft-spoken, Mr. Zheng said that every week, several hundred Fujianese immigrants from outside of New York return to his church for religious services. Monday and Wednesday are designed to serve immigrants returning from outside of New York because these workers are usually off on those two days.[22] The day we did our interview happened to be on a Monday in mid-August and we saw about two hundred immigrants attending the worship service. Each person signed in on a notebook at the front desk so that the church leaders would know how many people had come. Most take Chinatown buses to return to New York. Others who live further away may fly instead. The day we visited, Mr. Zheng said there was one immigrant who had arrived by air from Tennessee (spending $350 for the plane ticket). Another immigrant, who I greeted briefly as Pastor Zheng and I were in the lobby of the church, came from Minnesota.

During this interview with Mr. Zheng, I learned that Pastor Chen (who started the conference calls reported on by the *New York Times* in 2006) had retired and now lives in Dallas. Yet he continues to care deeply about the religious lives of the thousands of immigrant workers who are away from New York City. Pastor Chen tries as much as possible to visit restaurants in different states (within reasonable driving distance) to help immigrants understand the Bible and answer questions about religion.

These immigrants who work outside of NYC often return to see doctors, seek advice on legal matters, or simply to visit friends in Chinatown. Most of the returnees are restaurant workers (some are immigrant entrepreneurs) living in cities along the I-95 corridor. While in New York City, they always come to attend religious services. The second major religious linkage, perhaps most important for immigrants outside of New York City, is through We-Chat groups. There are more than 10 We-Chat groups for Bible study associated with members of this church alone. It should be noted that these We-Chat groups are organized by church members voluntarily, as opposed to being organized by church leaders. Church leaders kept reminding me about this point. One possible reason for the lack of support for We-Chat groups among church leaders is that church leaders prefer that immigrants come to the church and study the Bible in a traditional way. But times have changed. Social media is an important part of everyone's life. There are religion-based We-Chat groups for such subgroups as women and second-generation immigrants. Often, these groups are established by local New York–based members. Once they are established, however, they can easily break down geographical boundaries and accommodate restaurant workers from anywhere in the United States. It is quite often the case that someone with many years of experience studying the Bible can serve as a We-Chat group leader (*qun zhu*). Some of the elderly Christians are very active because they have more time and a more flexible schedule. But perhaps the most important role of such a We-Chat group is that it breaks traditional barriers separated by physical distance so that anyone anywhere can join the discussion. I joined one of the We-Chat groups and found that now I also have access to videos of their religious services on YouTube or in real time through Zoom.

I made an appointment at this church with the help of church leader Mr. Zheng to better understand how restaurant workers maintain involvement with religious groups in New York City even as they work and live elsewhere. When we arrived around noon, church sisters and brothers[23] were having lunch. As a courtesy, we were also kindly offered a simple lunch. My student and I interviewed two church members who belong to the same We-Chat group. Ms. Lin is an immigrant worker who came to the United States with her family when she was a small child. In 2010, she began attending the Church of Grace to the Fujianese due in part to her mother's mental health condition. Her first job was in upstate New York, about one and a half hours from New York City. At that time, she commuted to Chinatown to attend religious services every Wednesday, when she was off from work. She said she knows sisters and brothers in this Manhattan church well and did not mind the round-trip bus ride. Several years ago, her relatives who own a restaurant in a suburb of Philadelphia needed people to work for them, so she decided to move. Right now, it takes three hours to travel from her home near Philadelphia to the church in Manhattan. She still comes to this church every Monday, when she regularly has the day off. I asked her why she didn't just go to the church in Philadelphia instead of returning to New York. Her explanation was that she knows a lot of people in the Manhattan congregation and really feels comfortable with the church on Allen Street.

When Lin is not in New York, she uses We-Chat to maintain connections. We talked to Ms. Tong who is the We-Chat group leader (*qun zhu*). Tong said there are 113 members in this We-chat group. Over 50 percent are from outside New York City. Most of them used to live in New York before moving to other states. Each day, Bible passages are posted to the We-Chat group, typically by a senior member. Then, everybody can jump in to share thoughts, comments, or questions. Sometimes, a We-Chat group member who has encountered challenges in life or work will ask the other group members to pray for them. Unlike with the conference call format, a We-Chat group is very flexible. For example, immigrant workers are often very busy, making it difficult to find a time for everybody to meet for Bible study. So, telephone conference calls for Bible study are rather limited in terms of being able to reach a larger number of immigrant workers. A We-Chat group is especially good for restaurant workers with tight workday schedules because they can post or join the discussion any time when they have a free moment. They also receive (like I did) access to videos of church services in Chinatown that they can watch whenever it is convenient. We-Chat groups also have a social media tool that allows a subset of group members to hold a quick video chat if an important issue arises. I later learned that this We-Chat group is very active in that there are always new posts each day, especially at night. In general, women are more active than men in We-Chat group discussions.

Now let's look at the story in Philadelphia. Several years ago, when I visited the Church of Grace to Fujianese in that city, I interviewed Pastor Huang. I remember him telling me about his conference call that started at 11:30 p.m. I was quite moved by this at the time because 11:30 p.m. is bedtime for most people, but Pastor Huang still had to work. Huang said that about five years before, the conference call for Bible study had been replaced by We-Chat groups. At the time, there were eight or ten We-Chat groups dedicated to Bible study based out of the Philadelphia church. Pastor Huang is personally involved in seven We-Chat groups. He said that, for the most part, he reads posts on the groups and answers Bible-related questions. He is particularly diligent in communicating with new We-Chat members in order to facilitate discussion/questions about the Bible or beyond. According to Pastor Huang, 80 percent of the chat group members are located in New York, Philadelphia, or New Jersey. Another 10 percent of the group members live else-where along the East Coast and the remaining 10 percent live in other states.

This chapter is one of the first efforts to examine the continuing linkages between immigrants in NYC and those in new destinations. I argue that despite the increase of Chinese immigrant settlement in new destinations, Chinatown continues to play an important role in immigrants' lives. Theoretically, I advocate for the concept of trans-local immigrant entrepreneurship because it best characterizes the lives of these Chinese immigrants. This promising concept identifies a rising class of immigrant business owners and immigrant workers whose lives straddle two locations. I have elaborated three kinds of ties that connect immigrants in other states to Chinatown in Man-hattan: economic ties, social ties, and religious ties. I find that eco-nomic and religious ties are especially strong. Social media is now a very important part of everybody's lives, immigrants included. In this case, it seems that using social media such as We-Chat is a very effective way to build and maintain religious ties for immigrants who settle in non-gateway destinations. It is fair to say that Manhattan's Chinatown continues to be a hub for Chinese immigrant economic activities and a center for guiding immigrants' religious lives even when the immigrants themselves are physically located hundreds of miles away. Echoing recent studies of social life in the digital era by psychologist Sherry Turkle,[24] I find that many Chinese immigrants in new destinations are "alone" but also together, linked by Chinatown bus service, employment agencies, services provided by the China-town business community, and very active We-Chat groups.

7 Conclusion

Since the 1990s, the spatial diversification of immigrants from traditional destinations to new destinations has been widely noted.[1] The Chinese are no exception. Whereas thirty years ago, Chinese immigrants mainly clustered in major cities such New York, Chicago, San Francisco, and Los Angeles, they are now found all over the country, from North Creek in New York to Bur in Montana. In this book, I have tried to explain the trend of spatial dispersion among low-skilled Chinese immigrants.

If readers have traveled with me this far on this journey, I think most of you will have seen that Chinese immigrants' spatial relocation is quite distinctive on several fronts. Examples include the use of employment agencies for job searches, the creation of new transportation infrastructure (Chinatown buses) on which immigrant workers have come to rely, and the continuing connections between New York City's Chinatown and immigrants and entrepreneurs in new destinations. In this concluding chapter, I want to summarize key findings but also go beyond that to explore some of the theoretical and policy implications of these findings. I will focus on three aspects: the theoretical implication of the spatial dispersion of Chinatown workers, the new challenges for immigrant workers, and the future of Manhattan's Chinatown. In discussing these issues, it is also important to consider the impact of COVID-19 and recent anti-Asian violence on Chinatown's economy, immigrant workers, and entrepreneurs.

THE SPATIAL DISPERSION OF CHINESE IMMIGRANTS AND THEORETICAL IMPLICATIONS

First, this book proposes a new theoretical model of the spatial dispersion of Chinese immigrants to new destinations. Much of the literature on new destinations compares various outcomes for immigrants in new and traditional destinations without providing a clear understanding of the process by which this spatial dispersion takes place. The theoretical framework in chapter 1 (see figure 1.1) takes several key factors into account: employment agencies, Chinatown buses, and the supply chain of businesses based in Chinatown. This perspective moves away from the assumption that spatial assimilation is an individual level outcome.[2] Although individual immigrant entrepreneurs and workers may be motivated to move to new destinations, it is important to realize that this process is facilitated by other key institutions. This perspective supports the notion that entrepreneurship is an individual behavior, but also reflects group-level dynamics.[3]

Second, this book also challenges several notions about immigrants in the labor market. Many previous immigration scholars have argued that immigrant entrepreneurs select locations that are close to immigrant neighborhoods. The simple logic is that immigrant entrepreneurs rely on these neighborhoods for a supply of workers and customers of the same ethnic group. The story of Chinese immigrant entrepreneurs reveals that the conventional wisdom needs to be modified. The first priority from the Chinese entrepreneurs' per-spective is whether these locations make for good business markets that can generate enough demand and profits. The physical distance between Chinatown and new destinations for businesses is not insur-mountable in the twenty-first century because immigrants' businesses are supported by a network of employment agencies and a transporta-tion network of Chinatown buses. At the same time, the expansion of Chinese entrepreneurs into non-traditional destinations also implies that the Chinese restaurant business is a national labor market instead of a regional labor market, as is conceptualized by some mainstream scholars.[4]

From the immigrant business perspective, the traditional pattern of mom-and-pop operations is mainly a survival strategy. The new business model is more akin to a modern franchise model. When immigrants want to open their restaurants anywhere in the country, there is a system of business support and supply, from standardized decor and menus to three key players (employment agencies, bus companies, and supply shops) all located in Manhattan's China-town. This is what prompted former *New York Times* reporter Jen-nifer 8. Lee to use the term "open-source Chinese restaurant."[5] This system allows ambitious entrepreneurs to open more businesses with relative ease, moving the restaurant business from a survival strategy to a franchise model akin to that of McDonald's or KFC.[6] Unlike McDonald's and KFC though, which collect franchise fees from entrepreneurs, the Chinese immigrant model does not involve additional fees because it is not a brand owned by any corporation.

Third, as I observed immigrant entrepreneurs and immigrant workers moving to faraway locations, I wondered if this physical mobility could also lead to socio-economic mobility. For immigrant entrepreneurs, this is certainly the case, because the establishment of a new business often means a transition from worker to business owner. During the course of this project, I also found that sometimes the transition involved that from being a single-business owner to a multiple-business owner, as some Chinese immigrant entrepreneurs continue to expand their business interests. This is clearly another departure from the typical conception of immigrant business as a survival strategy.[7] In fact, it is not unusual to hear that immigrant entrepreneurs own two or more restaurants. James Li, who owns a cookware supply store in Chinatown, told us that he often deals with customers who have more than ten restaurants.

The 1980s and 1990s witnessed a lively debate on "ethnic enclaves."[8] These are often defined as a separate category of labor market (between a primary and secondary labor market) that has a strong immigrant character.[9] Some obvious examples of ethnic enclaves are Chinatowns in New York and San Francisco, as well as Little Havana in Miami. The two camps in this debate center on the idea of whether working in an ethnic enclave is a dead-end job choice or a possible springboard for socio-economic mobility.

After many years of research on this subject, the jury is still out. My research suggests two contributions for this debate. While I value the opportunity provided by the immigrant entrepreneurs working in New York's Chinatown, there is clearly a much bigger market outside of Chinatown. This larger outside market has done two key things for Chinese immigrants. It has allowed more immigrants to start their own businesses and become entrepreneurs. Owning one's own business is an immigrant's version of the American dream. And for immigrant workers, it increases their salary the moment they go to work outside of New York City. Thus, this study supports the thesis that "moving out" is "moving up." The mechanism for the economic gains for immigrants is really that the moment an immigrant broadens their job search beyond Chinatown, market forces become more important than the immigrant networks that may have given them their first job in Chinatown. In other words, immigrant entrepreneurs in new destinations have to offer more competitive market wages to attract immigrants to take these jobs. Second, unlike earlier studies that often suggest that an "enclave economy" benefits only the entrepreneurs, I find it is a win-win situation for both entrepreneurs and immigrant workers alike, as far as labor market outcomes are concerned.[10]

The final theoretical contribution of this book is the idea that assimilation is a two-way street. It is often taken for granted by classic assimilation theory that immigrants will gradually assimilate into American society in areas such as language, occupations, and neighborhood attainment. In recent years, many scholars have come to the conclusion that the other side of the story is increasingly true as well: immigrants have also changed American society.[11] Recent work by Jiménez gives us a telling case study in California.[12] My book provides a dose of new evidence in this direction, namely, the story of the Chinatown buses. Chinatown buses caught the attention of *Wall Street Journal* editors in 2005, in a front-page article about Greyhound losing customers to Chinatown buses. Many observers have noted that bus travel was not that pleasant in the 1990s. People did not like Greyhound's bus terminal on the West Side of Manhattan because the air quality was not ideal and getting there involved navigating a great deal of traffic. People with money invariably preferred to travel in style on Amtrak or by air. Then the Chinatown buses came along, originally intended to serve Chinese immigrants who needed to travel to faraway locations.[13] Chinatown buses have several attractive features, such as the fact that they board right at the curbside instead of at a bus terminal. Additionally, while they added more service to some major destinations such as Boston or Philadelphia, they also reach some less well-known locations that are underserved or not served at all by mainstream bus companies. And of course, travel on Chinatown buses comes at prices that you cannot disregard.

To better compete, mainstream bus companies have learned from the Chinatown buses. Curbside parking, for example, is becoming a new normal for mainstream inter-city bus transportation. The big bus company Megabus (now owned by Greyhound) picks up passengers on 34th Street (between 11th and 12th Avenues) in Manhattan. In Albany, the city where I live, Megabus picks up passengers curbside at Collins Circle on the campus of the State University of New York. Two days before Thanksgiving in 2021, I saw buses from four different companies parked along Collins Circle. On a recent trip to give a presentation, I saw buses from major bus companies parked curbside near the University of Pennsylvania in Philadelphia. The list goes on and on. Today, it is clear that the inter-city bus business is booming, in no small part because the big bus companies have picked up some tips from Chinatown bus operations.[14] David Wong, the owner of Eastern Bus Company, agreed: "I think Chinatown buses have really made a major contribution in changing the operating style of bus travel."

CHALLENGES FOR IMMIGRANTS AND THEIR FAMILIES

Although immigrants are likely to enjoy higher salaries by working in new destinations, this decisive shift in geographic location for employment presents some challenges for immigrants and their families. First, by definition, immigrants in these new destinations do not have easy access to immigrant organizations when they encounter practical difficulties such as driving tests, healthcare access, and a lack of church services in their native language. This is particularly challenging for recently arrived immigrants who do not speak English very well. Second, since these Chinese immigrants often work long hours in non-gateway destinations (typically twelve hours a day, six days a week), they are far away from their immigrant networks, often based in New York City, which could provide friendship and moral support. In these circumstances, immigrants are highly vulnerable to mental health issues that deserve our attention.[15] Third, immigration scholars also study potential racial conflicts between local residents and immigrants in new destinations. Our study suggests that Chinese immigrants and entrepreneurs are generally well-received and some Chinese restaurant owners also hire Latino and local white workers. In our ongoing work in northern Philadelphia, the situation is less rosy. These are neighborhoods with high concentrations of minority residents, high rates of unemployment and poverty, and a high proportion of single-parent families. Running a restaurant in this kind of environment can be dangerous. In the first week of August 2016, twelve Chinese restaurants were robbed at gunpoint.[16] Most restaurant owners in the area have installed bulletproof windows and security cameras. Perhaps this is not news to immigration scholars; however, the potential race and ethnic conflict needs more attention and research.[17]

Finally, based on our fieldwork, we have seen that some immigrant workers leave family members in New York while they move from job to job out of state. This clearly generates additional stress for immigrant families, especially those with children. Thus, moving to new immigrant destinations may prove to be a mixed blessing for some families. To the extent that the immigration labor market is quickly expanding to non-traditional destinations, scholars and policymakers need to find ways to facilitate immigrant adaptation in these destinations and resolve potential issues related to these new types of fragile immigrant families.

THE IMPACT OF COVID-19 ON CHINATOWN AND BEYOND

Having written this final chapter in the fall of 2021, it has been hard not to mention the impact of COVID-19 on Chinatown and new destinations. In fact, Chinatown felt the impact of COVID-19 much earlier than the rest of New York City, as people began avoiding Chinatown after learning that the new illness had originated in Wuhan, China. As New York became the first city in the United States to experience lockdown, tourists, customers, and some local residents fled the city, making it inevitable that Chinatown businesses suffered. According to Wellington Z. Chen, the executive director of the Chinatown Business Improvement District/Partnership, seventeen restaurants (out of over three hundred) permanently closed and 139 ground floor stores closed.[18] One of the most iconic restaurants in Chinatown, Jinfeng Restaurant, closed in March 2021. Before the pandemic, a typical week would bring Jinfeng Restaurant over ten thousand customers. Another major restaurant, 88 Palace (*Yidong Dajiulou*), closed even earlier, in September 2020.[19] Although business for 88 Palace was declining before COVID-19 due to the spatial dispersion of Fujianese immigrants, the emergence of COVID-19 dealt the final blow. The closing of 88 Palace was, for many immigrants, quite personal and emotional because the restaurant was often the first place where they had met their friends and relatives upon arriving in New York City. I also conducted many interviews with immigrant workers and attended social events in this restaurant sponsored by immigrant associations.

Beyond Chinatown, we can detect the impacts on other Chinese immigrant-owned businesses. I compared job postings in the Chinese language newspaper, "The World Journal" using data from July 25, 2019 and July 25, 2020. These job postings cover jobs in New York City as well as in other states. Overall, the number of job postings dropped by 55 period during that year, and all states with job listings saw a drop of some sort.[20] Immigrant entrepreneurs are facing new frontiers in terms of business. I conducted some additional interviews after the arrival of COVID-19 and noted some new business practices. One thing is clear: as with the country as a whole, online ordering from Chinese restaurants is increasing. That means business owners need to rely on big companies such as DoorDash and Uber Eats in order to increase their business volume. One restaurant owner summarized these effects, saying, "50 percent of my business now comes from online orders. Because of this new shift, I have to monitor online reviews to make sure about what people like and don't like. With online ordering becoming more prevalent, I do not need as many waiters as I used to." Another restaurant owner mentioned a bright spot during this tough time, namely that due to students learning from home (and eating lunch at home), there has been an uptick in online lunch orders from local families.

The rise of online ordering also has implications for the labor market demand for workers. The increase in online ordering means less demand for servers who are mainly needed for indoor dining. Restaurant owners reported that in this era of COVID-19, workers tend to stay put and not move around (even though that means missing some good opportunities). In a normally functioning labor market, when a worker quits their job, it opens a new position that needs to be advertised. However, if there are many workers who stay put, job market transitions tend to stall, and that will show up in the quantity of job postings as well.

The COVID-19 period of the last two years has also seen a steady rise in anti-Asian violence in major cities, from Atlanta to San Francisco to New York.[21] Jason Wang, CEO of Xi'an Famous Food (with fourteen branches in New York City), reported that two of his employees were punched in the nose either on the way to work or going home.[22] I contacted some of our informants recently to discuss the difficulties of operating in the shadow of COVID-19. One business owner had an unpleasant experience: a customer, while ordering a meal, mentioned that "we got COVID-19 from China." Another business owner who owns several properties and rents to local residents told us that one day, when he went to collect rent, an old white lady yelled at him, "Do not bring the virus to this community." Other more friendly neighbors came by and asked him to ignore her, which he did. While it is fortunate that none of our informants experienced violence firsthand, the anti-Asian violence/bias and its consequences are real and must be dealt with.

THE END OF CHINATOWN IN MANHATTAN?

Many scholars and commentators have made predictions about the future of Chinatown. Writing in the post-World War II era, sociologist Rose Lee remarked, "It appears that the number of Chinatowns in this country will decrease almost to the vanishing point. Only those of historical or commercial importance, as in San Francisco and New York will remain."[23] While this sounds alarming, it has proven to be inaccurate, as is evident from the booming of China-towns in the post-1965 era as changes in immigration law caused growing numbers of East Asian immigrants, among others, to arrive in the United States. In the last ten years or so, a few more commen-tators have joined the group of doomsayers pondering the future of Chinatowns. Bonnie Tsui, a long time Chinatown observer and author of an influential book on America's Chinatowns, asked in a 2011 issue of *The Atlantic* if we are seeing the end of Chinatown in the United States.[24] Tsui's argument is that with China's global rise to prominence, many immigrants have decided to return to China to pursue their Chinese dream, instead of the American dream.

A recent report in 2019, using studies of Chinatowns in Boston, Philadelphia, and New York, also noted a trend of decline, mainly brought on by the forces of gentrification.[25] Both arguments have a point considering data from the US Census Bureau about the popu-lation of Chinatown. For the first time, the 2010 census saw a decline in the population of Chinatown in Manhattan. Though the magni-tude of the decline (about 2 percent) is not enormous, the trend is unmistakable. Since then, the Chinatown population has continued to decline. If we look at the Chinese population in Chinatown in Manhattan, the decline is even more striking. Figure 7.1 shows the changes in Chinese population in two Chinatown zip codes in Man-hattan. The Chinese population experienced a 13 percent decline from 2000 to 2010. The Chinese population reached its lowest point of 37,420 in 2016. Clearly, the decline in the population of China-town is driven by the decline in the Chinese population living there.

My own fieldwork experience in Chinatown corroborates this story. When I first started working in Manhattan's Chinatown in the early 2000s, business was really bustling. Any reasonable space that you could find in Chinatown would be rented out. On East Broad-way alone, you could see over twenty shops selling telephone cards to immigrants. This was an era before iPhones and also before free social

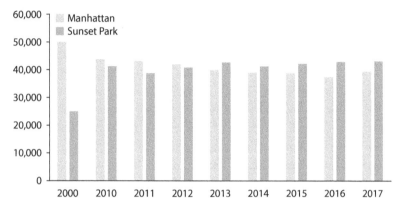

Figure 7.1. Changes in the Chinese population in two Chinatowns in New York City, 2000–2017.

media communication options such as We-Chat. Today, there are many "For Rent" signs on East Broadway (especially in the aftermath of COVID-19), suggesting a possible change of tide in Chinatown.

Although Tsui's observation is generally correct, then, the reasons for this decline are more complicated than she suggested in 2011. The rise of economic prosperity in China has contributed to Chinatown's possible decline, but there are more factors at play here. This book reveals that larger numbers of Chinese immigrants (especially younger ones) have moved to other states to start new businesses or find work offering higher pay. There is also a tendency for Chinese immigrants (especially low-skilled immigrants from Fujian province) to move to Sunset Park in Brooklyn and, to a lesser extent, to Flushing in Queens. As we moved toward the last decade of the twentieth century and the first decade of the twenty-first century, many immigrants found themselves ready to get married and start families. But for this group, Chinatown in Manhattan is simply too expensive to support families with children. Thus, moving to Brooklyn's Sunset Park, where housing prices are much more affordable, is a natural decision. As we watched the decline in Manhattan's Chinatown population from 2000 to 2010, the population in Sunset Park experienced a very dramatic increase of 63 percent (from 25,264 in 2000 to 41,169 in 2010). By 2017, according to data from American Community Survey, the Chinese population in Sunset Park reached its peak of 42,789.

Any visitor to Sunset Park today will see an extremely vibrant Chinese immigrant community with bustling businesses of all kinds. It is similar to the variant economy of East Broadway during the 2000s. Walking along 8th Avenue where the majority of Chinese businesses are located, we see a lot of young families with children—a much bigger crowd of Chinese immigrants compared to Manhattan's Chinatown. New York's politicians have also taken notice. I participated in a Chinese New Year celebration in February 2015 and saw more than ten politicians (including Sen. Chuck Schumer, a long-time friend to immigrants) from New York State and New York City join the celebration/performances and show of firecrackers. A whole block of 8th Avenue was closed to all traffic. Certainly, today's Sunset Park rivals Manhattan's Chinatown in some respects.

The final factor in this story is the force of gentrification. Along East Broadway, there has been a facelift of sorts, apparent anywhere you go. There is a new mainstream hotel, a Fairfield Inn and Suites (by Marriott), at the intersection of Henry Street and East Broadway. Another signature building is the fourteen-story Boutique Office Condo (100 East Broadway), which replaced a gas station. The most expensive units in this building come with a price tag above $5 million for more than 6,000 square feet of space. In addition to the big players, plenty of small boutique shops and eateries, such as Brazilian bakeries, and trendy bars have popped up as well. Rest assured, the rent will continue to be high in this environment, especially for immigrant workers who want to start families.

So far, I have provided a more thorough explanation of the decline of Chinatown's population in recent years. The real question though, is whether Chinatown is declining to such an extent that it is in danger of fading away. Analysis from the previous chapter suggests that the answer is definitely no. I argue that despite the declining population of Chinese who reside there, Chinatown is likely to continue to be a vibrant community. Beyond Chinatown's own business landscape of more than three hundred restaurants, shops, and a rising upscale service economy (as reflected in fancy hotels, high rise buildings, spa and skin care, and countless jewelry shops), it serves as a hub that links Chinese immigrant businesses across large parts of the country and the vast Chinese immigrant workforce. Chinatown is home to numerous employment agencies that circulate the immigrant workforce. It is the anchor of a supply chain network that provides service for a booming restaurant industry across the whole country. The neighborhood fosters many social ties that link immigrants who share hometown origins and other social identities (such as religion). The Chinatown bus system provides the necessary transportation infrastructure to facilitate all of these linkages for Chinese immigrants who work in different parts of the country. In fact, Willington Chen, the executive director of the Chinatown planning council, says that these buses bring about 4 million people to Chinatown each year. Of course, Chinatown will continue to be a major tourist destination for global and domestic travelers, especially when New York City is fully recovered from Covid-19. That, in turn, brings a lot of dynamism to Chinatown's economy now and will continue to do so in the future.

As if I have not shown enough of a sense of optimism so far, the support from the State of New York for Manhattan's Chinatown reached a new high on November 10, 2021, when Governor Kathy Hochul announced a $20 million grant for the revitalization of Chinatown. Among its proposed projects is to turn the well-known restaurant 88 Palace (*Yidong Dajiulou*), which closed in September 2020, into a cultural and performance center. The award of this grant at this critical moment when Chinatown seemed at its lowest point has created a high level of excitement among community leaders, business owners, and workers in Chinatown and in new immigrant destinations. It also solidifies the notion that Manhattan's Chinatown is an American cultural and economic institution that will maintain its vibrancy for a long time to come.[26] In this regard, perhaps it is appropriate to end this book with Gov. Hochul's upbeat remarks at the grant-award ceremony in November: "Chinatown serves as a beacon of cultural richness and diversity, not just for New Yorkers, *but for the entire world.*" She continued, "With this award, Chinatown will shine even brighter and reach its fullest potential as a vibrant community and an international arts and cultural destination."[27]

APPENDIX A Methods

Data used in this paper are from three surveys and interviews:

(1) Two surveys of employment agencies in Manhattan
(2) A survey of immigrant entrepreneurs in six states in the United States
(3) Additional interviews with a variety of immigrants, church leaders, owners of Chinatown bus companies, employment agencies, and other entrepreneurs

SURVEYS OF EMPLOYMENT AGENCIES

In September 2010, we surveyed employment agencies (EAs) in Manhattan's Chinatown. EAs are mainly located on Eldridge Street, Division Street, and East Broadway on the Lower East Side of Manhattan. Some informants call East Broadway "Fuzhou Street" to represent the large number of immigrants from Fujian province. The geographic concentration of these EAs is not random, but emerged because they initially wanted to serve the employment needs of Fujianese immigrants. Today EAs also serve employment needs for Latino workers. Before we started fieldwork, the author talked to owners or staff members of EAs to get their permission for our data collection. One EA refused to participate. In September 2010, we surveyed eleven EAs out of the thirty-two located in Manhattan's

Chinatown that we were able to identify at the time. For each EA, a team of graduate students recorded job-related information including location (determined by telephone area code), salary level, type (chef or food delivery), work hours, type of restaurant (most were Chinese, but a few served Japanese food) and any other pertinent information (such as how tips are distributed, or any preference for immigrants who came from different parts of China). We gathered information on 2,147 jobs. To capture potential seasonal variations on the job market, we repeated this process in February 2011 with a new random sample of eleven EAs. Information on 2,316 jobs was gathered during the second survey.

SURVEY OF IMMIGRANT ENTREPRENEURS IN NEW DESTINATIONS

The 2014 survey focused exclusively on Chinese immigrant entrepreneurs in new destinations. In total, thirty-six Chinese immigrant entrepreneurs were selected from six states (Florida, North Carolina, Ohio, Pennsylvania, Texas, and Virginia), with six entrepreneurs selected in each state. Two methods of data collection were used to select these entrepreneurs. The specific locations were selected based on job advertisements posted in employment agencies in Manhattan's Chinatown. We selected locations that had a growing presence in the job advertisements, so that the interviewers would be able to find Chinese business owners once they arrived. To select immigrant entrepreneurs in each location, we first relied on religious networks to identify Chinese immigrant entrepreneurs in the six states. Because a very high proportion of Chinese immigrants (especially immigrants from Fujian province) are religious, using religious connections is an effective way to identify immigrant entrepreneurs. The second way we identified Chinese immigrant entrepreneurs (restaurant owners in most cases) was by using Google Maps. Once a location in one of the six states was selected, we used Google Maps to list all Chinese restaurants within fifty miles of that location. Then we randomly called each restaurant on the list until the target sample size was reached. In addition to administering a standard questionnaire, the interviewers also conducted in-depth interviews with at least two business owners in each state.

We also carried out in-depth-interviews with a variety of other immigrant workers and entrepreneurs over the years. For one survey we interviewed ten immigrant workers, some of whom were in Chinatown looking for work, who shared their experiences with employment agencies and working in new destinations, while others were in various locations outside of New York. We interviewed three owners and staff member of Chinatown bus companies, three owners of employment agencies, and four owners of restaurant supply store owners in Chinatown. We have also interviewed church leaders in Sunset Park in Brooklyn, Chinatown in Manhattan, Philadelphia, one social media We-Chat group leader in Manhattan, and immigrant workers attending church services. To study the impact of COVID-19 on immigrant workers and entrepreneurs, between December 2020 and November 2021, we interviewed four business owners and five workers who shared with us their experiences in the context of COVID-19 and anti-Asian violence.

APPENDIX B   Analysis of Job Locations

STATISTICAL MODELS OF LOCATION CHOICES OF CHINESE RESTAURANTS USING AREA CODE ZONING DATA

To assess the potential impact of imprecision between area codes and the counties whose attributes were mapped onto the area codes, we created an indicator (dummy) variable, scored 1 if the area code polygon fully enveloped its component counties, and 0 otherwise, and included this as a control variable in each of our regression models. None of the dummy variables was statistically significant. We then refit the regressions without the dummy variable and compared the estimated coefficients, standard errors, and test statistics. None of the statistical inference differed between models with and without the dummy variable, so we report the models without the dummy control for area code to component county mismatch.

Following the procedure described above, we obtained an area code zone level data file with the distribution of Chinese restaurant jobs as well as basic economic, business, and crime data at the area code level.[1]

Our outcome of interest is the number of jobs in an area code zone. However, to use information from both (2010 and 2011) surveys (see Appendix A), we averaged the number of jobs in each area code over two years. The resulting averaged counts are not always integers; however, the number of jobs can reasonably be assumed to be randomly drawn from each area code's Poisson distribution with a single parameter, λ, determining the properties of that distribution. This parameter, λ, may be interpreted as an area code's job listing rate of occurrence or propensity over a given period.[2]

In addition, our data collection of job listings likely involves noisy measurement that introduces random variation into λ_i, thereby altering the Poisson formulation by building in a second source of uncertainty.[3] This leads us to utilize the negative binomial distribution. While we agree with Berk and MacDonald that the negative binomial regression model (NBRM) is overused for count data and misunderstood as an all-purpose "fix" to excess variation in the conditional distribution of count data, our application appears to be justified by an expectation of excess variation in the stochastic part of the model.

Accordingly, we can write the NBRM with the rate, μ_i, as a function of observed $x_k s$ and a disturbance term (as in a normal regression) that reflects unobserved heterogeneity among the observations:

$$\ln \mu_i = \boldsymbol{x}_i^T \boldsymbol{\beta} + \varepsilon_i$$

Exponentiating both sides yields

$$\mu_i = \exp(\boldsymbol{x}_i^T \boldsymbol{\beta}) \exp(\varepsilon_i) = \exp(\boldsymbol{x}_i^T \boldsymbol{\beta}) \delta_i$$

where we define $\delta = \exp(\varepsilon)$ and then assume that δ is drawn from a gamma distribution and normalized so that the expected value $E(\delta) = 1$.[4]

Our NBRM draws on several literatures to specify the systematic part of the model. Drawing from the economic sociology of immigration,[5] we expect that higher counts of job listings are more likely to be in Asian/Chinese immigrant-concentrated places; therefore, our model includes measures for the proportion of total population that is non-Hispanic white, non-Hispanic black, and Asian. As mentioned earlier, we are not able to specifically measure the Chinese proportion of total population in each area code, so we use the Asian proportion as a close proxy. The "transition zones" perspective from human ecological theory predicts that immigrant businesses and jobs are located in transition zones with high social disorganization and crime rates. Alternatively, the "business climate" perspective advocated by economists suggests that immigrant businesses and jobs are more likely located in places with low unemployment, low crime rates, and an established business climate.[6] Accordingly, our regressions include median household income, the unemployment rate, the property crime rate, and the number of businesses in the accommodation and food sectors. We also control for population size (population and population-squared) and the geographic size of the area code zone (square miles). Our decision to allow for nonlinearity between the number of jobs and population size is motivated by our pre-regression observation of a positive association that holds until the area code population size surpasses four million, after which the association becomes negative. Although there are not many cases with such a large population and our ability to theorize about them is not sufficiently developed, there are enough such cases to suggest that the negative association is real and that our model specification should allow for this functional form.

We also consider that controlling for the size of area code zones is not sufficient to eliminate the impact of spatial heterogeneity. Indeed, our analysis reveals the large disparity in the size of US area codes. Many states in the North Central, West, and Southwest regions have only one or a few area codes, while states in the East, South, and Central regions are highly subdivided. Studies have documented spatial dependence between area units in regression-based analyses. For example, Crowder and South considered the influence of extra-local conditions on white flight in the context of residential mobility research.[7] Both extra-local conditions and economic activity in any region that borders the focal unit may impact the conditions within the focal unit. Of primary concern to this study, the number of job listings in an area code may be correlated with job listings in nearby or adjacent area codes because immigrant entrepreneurs may open restaurants near other successful restaurants. Even under the best circumstances, a maximum-likelihood (ML) estimator of spatial dependence is not well-suited to probability models, including models for count data, and when coupled with severe disparity in the size of areal units, the conditions necessary for model convergence are rarely met.

We address the potential for spatial heterogeneity and a specific form for spatial dependence by including state fixed effects (a vector of dummy variables that uniquely identifies each state). Our approach is motivated by the observation that highly subdivided states will have more within-state than between-state area code "neighbors," while states with only one or few area codes have such large area code zone sizes that between-state spatial dependence is an unlikely consequence.

SUPPLEMENTARY MODELS OF THE EARNINGS
OF IMMIGRANT WORKERS

To examine how the spatial location of jobs relates to wages for immigrant workers, we estimate two additional types of models. The first uses jobs as the unit of analysis and estimates multilevel models using information about jobs as the first level and information about job location (area code) as the second level.[8] The advantage of this approach is that we estimate how certain job characteristics are related to wages, in addition to how our key interest in distance from New York City is related to wages. Since we are using characteristics for each job, we can use either our 2010 or 2011 survey of EAs. We decided to use the 2011 survey for this purpose.[9]

Our second strategy estimates conventional spatial lag and spatial error regression models using area code as the unit of analysis and the mean monthly wage at the area code level as our dependent variable (again using the 2011 EA survey data) and other area code level variables as predictor variables.[10]

Following Anselin[11] and Chi and Zhu[12], we estimate the following spatial lag model with a "queen" contiguity spatial weights matrix:

$$Y = X\beta + \lambda WY + \varepsilon$$

Here Y denotes the logged mean monthly salary for jobs listed in each area code, X represents a matrix of exogenous explanatory variables at the area code level, WY introduces endogeneity in the outcome by connecting neighboring area codes, and ε is the error term. We also estimate a spatial error model in the following form:

$$\ln \mu_i = \boldsymbol{x}_i^T \boldsymbol{\beta} + \varepsilon_i \text{ and } \ln \mu_i = \boldsymbol{x}_i^T \boldsymbol{\beta} + \varepsilon_i$$

where W_ε allows for unobserved correlated effects that are quantified in λ. For all wage related spatial models, we control for the cost of living along with selected area code level characteristics.

Table B.1 Estimated Coefficients from Negative Binomial Models of the Number of Jobs in an Area Code Zone

Independent variables	Model A		Model B*	
	B	SE	B	SE
Intercept	−6.7407***	0.7263	−27.1529***	1.7491
Non-Hispanic white percentage	0.0402***	0.0074	0.0274**	0.0093
Black percentage	0.0486***	0.0109	−0.0018	0.0149
Asian percentage	−0.2178***	0.0310	−0.2393***	0.0554
Population in the area code (in 100,000)	0.0539	0.0283	0.1397**	0.0438
Population in the area code (in 100,000) squared	−0.0010*	0.0004	−0.0013*	0.0005
Square miles of the area code (in 10,000)	0.1726*	0.0757	0.3685**	0.1131
Median household income				
Below $40,000			.5366*	0.6299
$40,000–$50,000			1.4818**	0.5434
$50,000–$60,000			1.2500*	0.5358
$60,000–$70,000			0.3491	0.4688
$70,000 or above (reference)			—	—
Unemployment proportion			−0.7654***	0.2290
Property crime rate			−0.0001*	0.0000
Number of establishments (in 1,000; food & accommodation)			−0.1537	0.1481
z-ratio of Moran's I statistic	11.166***		1.563	
Log likelihood	4685.0115		4766.2909	
AIC	1664.9960		1612.4373	

NOTE: * P < 0.05, ** P < 0.01 and *** P < 0.001
SOURCE: Liang et al., "From Chinatown to Everytown," Table 3.

Table B.2 Estimated Coefficients from Multi-level Model of Monthly Salary (logged)

Independent variables	Model A B	Model A SE	Model B* B	Model B* SE
Intercept	7.8633***	0.0865	7.9537***	0.0732
Job-level characteristics (by job category)				
Cook (reference)				
Server	—		0.0307***	0.0077
Delivery driver	—		−0.0131	0.0132
Others	—		−0.1848***	0.0069
Area code–level characteristics				
Distance from New York City	0.0112***	0.0012	0.0084***	0.0010
Asian percentage	−0.0034	0.0024	−0.0026	0.0020
Population in the area code (in 100,000)	0.0010	0.0006	0.0010*	0.0005
Square miles of the area code (in 10,000)	−0.0096	0.0068	−0.0056	0.0058
Percent of population in labor force	−0.0962	0.1504	−0.1982	0.1267
Cost of living/100	−0.0044	0.0028	−0.0021	0.0023
Unemployment proportion	0.0088	0.0066	0.0074	0.0056

NOTE: * $P < 0.05$, ** $P < 0.01$ and *** $P < 0.001$
SOURCE: Liang et al., "From Chinatown to Everytown," Table 4.

Table B.3 Estimated Coefficients from Spatial Models of Salary (logged) at the Area Code Level

Independent variables	Model A (spatial error model)		Model B* (spatial lag model)	
	B	SE	B	SE
Intercept	7.9525***	0.1151	7.9497***	0.1155
Distance from New York City	0.0001***	0.00002	0.0001***	0.00002
Asian percentage	–0.0053	0.0030	–0.0054	0.0030
Population in the area code (in 100,000)	0.0004	0.0006	0.0004	0.0006
Square miles of the area code (in 10,000)	–0.0085	0.0047	–0.0084	0.0048
Percent of population in labor force	–0.1556	0.1683	–0.1549	0.1683
Cost of living/100	–0.0008	0.0041	–0.0007	0.0041
Unemployment percentage	–0.0021	0.0070	–0.0021	0.0070
Lambda	0.00002	0.00007		
Rho	0.00002	0.00007		
Log likelihood	226.6569	226.6686		
z-ratio of Moran's I statistic	1.399	1.399		

NOTE: * P < 0.05, ** P < 0.01 and *** P < 0.001
SOURCE: Liang et al., "From Chinatown to Everytown," Table 5.

Notes

CHAPTER 1. INTRODUCTION

1. Chew and Liu, "Hidden in Plain Sight"; Liang and Zhou, "Legal Status."

2. Kinkead, *Chinatown*; Lin, *Reconstructing Chinatown*; Nee and Nee, *Chinatown*; Liang and Ye, "From Fujian to New York"; Zhou, *Chinatown*; Kwong, *The New Chinatown*; Tsui, *American Chinatown*.

3. The distribution of highly skilled Chinese immigrants has become less spatially constrained in recent decades, which should be treated separately.

4. Hilgers, "The Kitchen Networks."

5. B. Anderson, "With Chop and Suey."

6. Portes and Rumbaut, *Immigrant America*.

7. Loewen, *The Mississippi Chinese*; Ling, *Chinese St. Louis*. I thank an anonymous reviewer for making this suggestion. Also see Mendelson, *Chow Chop Suey*.

8. Fennelly, "Discrimination against Immigrants"; Marrow, *New Destinations Dreaming*.

9. Proposition 187 never went into effect because it was ruled unconstitutional in federal court. I thank an anonymous reviewer for noting

this. However, the larger context of passing Proposition 187 did display an unfriendly social environment for immigrants at the time.

10. Massey and Capoferro, "The New Geographic Diversification of U.S. Immigration."

11. Donato, Tolbert, Nucci, and Kawanno, "Changing Faces, Changing Places"; Hall and Crowder, "Native Out-Migration"; Kandel and Parrado, "Restructuring of the US Meat Processing Industry"; Lichter, Parisi, Taquino, and Grice, "Residential Segregation in New Hispanic Destinations"; Parrado and Kandel, "New Hispanic Migrant Destinations"; Leach and Bean, "The Structure and Dynamics."

12. Light, *Deflecting Immigration*.

13. Flippen and Kim, "Immigrant Context and Opportunity."

14. Office of Immigration Statistics, *2007 Yearbook*.

15. Massey and Denton, "Spatial Assimilation."

16. Liang, "Demography of Illicit Emigration."

17. Hilgers, "The Kitchen Networks"; Keef, "The Snakehead"; "China Villa Envy"; Lii, "The Chinese Menu Guys."

18. Portes and Rumbaut, *Immigrant America*.

19. Boswell, "A Split Labor Market".

20. Newman, "On the East Coast."

21. Liang and Zhou, "Legal Status and Labor Market and Health Consequences."

CHAPTER 2. JOB SEARCH

1. M. Zhou, "Diverse Origins and Destinies"; Hum, *Making A Global Immigrant Neighborhood*. Chinatown in Brooklyn refers to an area between 44th Street and 68th Street along 8th Avenue. There is a commuter bus that runs from Chinatown in Manhattan to 8th Avenue in Brooklyn and another running from Chinatown to Flushing. Most Chinese immigrants call the Chinatown in Brooklyn simply "the 8th Avenue."

2. Massey, "Why does Immigration Occur"; M. Zhou, *Chinatown*.

3. Waldinger, *Still the Promised City?*, 302.

4. A high proportion of Fujianese immigrants are undocumented. Many of them are able to get green cards by applying for asylum; see Liang, "The Rules of the Game," and Hsin and Aptekar, "The Violence of Asylum." During my interviews in different churches, some pastors mentioned that they had written supporting letters for some Fujianese immigrants' applications for asylum.

5. Figure 2.2 identifies the locations of all thirty-two employment agencies we used in our sample. Note that some locations contain more than one EA because another EA could be on a different floor in the same building, or one large office might contain two or three EAs.

6. Note that our online search of EAs in 2016 did not find EAs in Sunset Park, but when we did fieldwork in subsequent years, we did find some EAs in Sunset Park.

7. Despite a large number of Chinese immigrants who reside in Sunset Park in Brooklyn, there are only two EAs in figure 2.4. This reflects the fact that Chinatown in Brooklyn developed later than the ones in Manhattan and Queens. I also note there is a rising demand for Chinese restaurant jobs from non-Chinese immigrant workers. Among non-Chinese job seekers, most are Latino immigrants, though others come from Southeast Asia.

8. Dolnick, "Many Immigrants' Job Search"; Hilgers, *Patroit Number One.*

9. Dolnick, "Many Immigrants' Job Search."

10. See Appendix A for detailed discussion of our interviews with owners of EAs.

11. Lii, "Neighborhood Report."

12. This is clearly not a standard practice. In fact, all staff members we interviewed in EAs say that no money is given by employers.

13. Here we use the terms "good workers" and "good jobs" loosely. We want to convey the idea that both employers and workers have expectations about the job. Having talked to many employers and workers, we think for employers, "good workers" refers to those who work hard and are reliable. For immigrant workers, the most important feature of "good jobs" is that employers are honest and transparent about the nature of the job and expectations for work hours. One thing potential workers often complain about is that although the salary might seem attractive, they arrive to find out that the work is too grueling. Likewise, employers also complain that today's immigrant workers do not work as hard as earlier generations of immigrants.

14. Cao, "Immigrants Face Difficult Times."

15. Dolnick, "Many Immigrants' Job Search."

16. Shah, "Immigrants from China." The Census Bureau defines an "immigrant" as a foreign-born person who was in a foreign country one year earlier and was living in the United States at the time of the American Community Survey. For a fuller exposition of the history of Chinese

immigrants, see M. Zhou, *Chinatown*; Daniels, *Asian America*; Kwong and Miscevic, *Chinese America*.

17. US Census Bureau, "Tabulations from the 2013 American Community Survey."

18. Migration Policy Institute, Immigrants from Asia in the United States. The total number of Chinese immigrants would be nearly 2.9 million if we include the 372,000 immigrants from Taiwan.

19. Nee and Nee, *Longtime Californ'*; Sung, *Mountain of Gold*.

20. Wang, "Leaving China's North."

21. Trillin, "Have They Run Out of Provinces Yet."

22. Li, "*New Yorker* Writer"; Ramsy, "Calvin Trillin's Poem."

23. Li, "*New Yorker* Writer."

24. It took a significant amount of effort to locate data on Chinese immigrant hometown associations. Given that most immigrant associations are headquartered in large cities or states with large populations of Chinese immigrants, we focused on Chinese immigrant associations in New York City, Washington, DC, California, and Texas. We began the process by searching "同乡会", the Chinese term for "hometown association," in the context of selected locations. We looked through ten pages of search results looking for specific names of associations in each location. Sometimes we would find a useful link to an association's website and be able to obtain information on the year the association was established. Other times, we found websites listing Chinese immigrant associations in a selected location (such as Washington, DC). Then we would search for reports on the anniversary events associated with each Chinese immigrant association in that location because they might help us identify the year the association was established. For example, an immigrant association having a twentieth anniversary celebration in 2016 would have been established in 1996. When we could not find such information, we phoned or emailed the manager of the immigrant association to inquire about the year of the association's founding.

25. Hooper and Batalova, "Chinese Immigrants"; Liang and Song. "Migration in China"; Zhou, "Hillary Clinton Hosting Fund-Raising Dinner."

26. Granovetter, "Economic Sociology of Firms and Entrepreneurs." Granovetter's main finding is that people got important job information from casual acquaintances or new friends ("weak ties") rather than from old friends ("strong ties"). The logic is that it is often the case that old friends possess similar job-related information.

27. We were able to identify thirty-two employment agencies in Chinatown in 2011 (some of them are closed today).

28. Sanders and Nee, "Limits of Ethnic Solidarity."

29. Cao, "Immigrants Face Difficult Times ."

30. Wilson, "Bridging the Service Divide."

31. This survey was done in New York City as part of the binational survey of Chinese immigrants in the United States; also see Liang et al., "Cumulative Causation."

CHAPTER 3. MAKING THE CONNECTION

1. Newman, "On the East Coast."

2. See also Hilgers, "The Kitchen Networks."

3. Huang, "Artists Pay Tribute."

4. Ungerleider, "Business Lessons."

5. Klein, "Emergency Curbside."

6. I verified more than half of the companies in Chinatown during 2019 and interviewed some bus owners and staff members. The research was carried out prior to COVID-19, so some bus companies have temporarily or permanently discontinued services due to the pandemic.

7. Luo, "In Chinatown, a $10 Trip Means War."

8. Foner, *One Out of Three*; Reiss, "New York's Shadow Transit"; Summathi, "Illegal But Very Popular." The dollar van transportation business, like the rest of NYC public transportation, has been devastated by the COVID-19 pandemic; see Martinez, "Illegal Dollar Van Drivers."

9. Liang and Ye, "From Fujian to New York."

10. Chin, *Smuggled Chinese*; Keefe, "The Snakehead"; Kwong, *The Forbidden Workers;* Liang and Song, "Migration in China."

11. Liang et al., "Cumulative Causation."

12. Kain, "The Spatial Mismatch Hypothesis"; Mouw, "Are Black Workers Missing the Connection"; W. Wilson, *The Truly Disadvantaged*; Kasinitz and Rosenberg, "Missing the Connection."

13. W. Wilson, *The Truly Disadvantaged*.

14. It should be noted there are differences between the African American example in the spatial mismatch argument and the case of Chinese immigrant workers. In the case of African American job seekers, employing businesses are often owned by whites, while in the current case study business owners and job seekers are the same racial group. In addition, Chinese immigrant entrepreneurs clearly prefer to hire Chinese immigrant

workers in most cases, whereas the white business owners may or may not prefer African American workers. I thank one anonymous reviewer for this point.

15. NYC Department of City Planning, *Chinatown Bus Study*.

16. Fuchs, "Fung Wah Bus."

17. Newman, "On the East Coast."

18. Park and Burgess, "Introduction"; Thomas and Znaieck, *The Polish Peasants*; Gordon, "Assimilation."

19. Portes and Zhou, "The New Second Generation." This is not the place to have a fuller discussion of segmented assimilation, but briefly, it proposes three possible paths. The first path is more like the traditional assimilation trajectory. The second path is to assimilate but also maintain some elements of immigrants' own culture. The third path is clearly not predicted by the traditional assimilation theory, and involves downward assimilation for some groups.

20. Alba and Nee, *Remaking the American Mainstream*.

21. Alba and Nee, *Remaking the American Mainstream*.

22. Orum, "Circles of Influence."

23. Hirschman, "Immigration and the American Century."

24. Diaz and Ore, "Landscapes."

25. Jiménez, *The Other Side of Assimilation*, 11.

26. Jiménez, *The Other Side of Assimilation*; Jiménez and Horowitz, "When White is Just Alright."

27. Min, "Settlement Patterns"; Yoon, *On My Own*; Waldinger, *Through the Eye of the Needle*; Zhou, *Chinatown*.

28. Hirschman, "Immigration and the American Century."

29. Klein and Zitcer, "Everything"; Schwieterman et al., "The Remaking of the Motor Coach"; Meyer et al, *Deregulation*.

30. Chaddick Institute of Metropolitan Development, *Adding on Amenities*; Alba and Nee, *Remaking the American Mainstream*.

31. NYC Department of City Planning, Chinatown Bus Study; Xu, "Council Woman Margaret Chin and DOT Explain Bus Permit."

32. Lowy and Stamm, "The End of the Chinatown Bus?"

33. Chaddick Institute of Metropolitan Development, *Adding on Amenities*.

34. M. Li, "The Closing."

35. Eskebnazi and Kane, "Farewell."

36. A quick Google search will reveal massive numbers of postings by Chinatown bus passengers who share their experiences. Here is one that

may be representative of passengers' comments. "Every time you told someone that you've taken a trip on the Chinatown Bus, they'd be like, 'Oh, man, I have a story about that.'" "Once I started digging into some of the stories, I realized that there were so many, whether it's the bus breaking down and people arguing on the side of the highway, or just really random situations with random stops on the side of the road to drop off or pick up people." See Owen, "Anyone Who Has Ridden or Heard of the Chinatown Bus." Thanks to an anonymous reviewer who made this suggestion.

37. National Academy of Sciences, *Economic and Fiscal Impact of Immigration*. Thanks to an anonymous reviewer who suggested including this discussion of possible economic impacts of low-skilled immigrant workers and entrepreneurs.

38. Alba and Nee, *Remaking the American Mainstream*; Hirschman, Kastnitz, and DeWind, *Handbook*.

CHAPTER 4. CHOICES FOR NEW IMMIGRANT DESTINATIONS

1. Foner, *From Ellis Island to JFK*; Logan, Alba, and Zhang, "Immigrant Enclaves and Ethnic Communities in New York and Los Angeles"; Nee and Nee, *Longtime Californ'*; Nee, Sanders, and Sernau, "Job Transitions in an Immigrant Metropolis"; Portes and Bach, *Latin Journey*; Waters and Jiménez, "Assessing Immigrant Assimilation"; Zhou, *Chinatown*.

2. Massey, "The New Immigration"; Min, "Settlement Patterns and Diversity."

3. Singer calls some of the new destination cities "new immigrant gateways" (*The Rise of New Immigrant Gateways*, 5).

4. Singer, *The Rise of New Immigrant Gateways*. See also Goździak and Martin, *Beyond the Gateway*; Hirschman and Massey, "Places and Peoples"; Marrow, *New Destination Dreaming*; Massey, *New Faces in New Places*; Zuniga and Hernandez-Leon, *New Destinations*.

5. Flippen and Kim, "Immigrant Context and Opportunity."

6. Logan, Alba, and McNulty, "Ethnic Economies in Metropolitan Regions"; Portes, *The Economic Sociology of Immigration*.

7. Liang et al., "Cumulative Causation, Market Transition, and Emigration from China."

8. Portes, *The Economic Sociology of Immigration*.

9. Light and Bonacich, *Immigrant Entrepreneurs*; Light et al., "Beyond the Ethnic Enclave Economy"; Light and Rosenstein, "Expanding the Interaction Theory of Entrepreneurship."

10. Light and Bonacich, *Immigrant Entrepreneurs*.

11. Light et al., "Beyond the Ethnic Enclave Economy."

12. Granovetter, "The Economic Sociology of Firms and Entrepreneurs"; Geertz, "The Rotating Credit Association"; Portes and Sensenbrenner, "Embeddedness and Immigration." Recent reports suggest some rotation credit practices have failed and immigrants have suffered major financial losses in the Chinese community in New York City; China Qiaowang, "Chinese Immigrants Lost Millions."

13. Fong, Luk, and Ooka, "Spatial Distribution of Suburban Ethnic Businesses"; Sassen, "Immigration and Local Labor Markets"; Zhou, *Chinatown*.

14. Fong, Luk, and Ooka, "Spatial Distribution of Suburban Ethnic Businesses."

15. Scott, *Metropolis*.

16. Yu Zhou, "Beyond Ethnic Enclaves."

17. W. Li, "Anatomy of a New Ethnic Settlement"; W. Li, "Los Angeles' Chinese Ethnoburb"; Yu Zhou, "Beyond Ethnic Enclaves."

18. Card and Lewis, "The Diffusion of Mexican Immigrants."

19. Massey mentions this in passing in *New Faces and New Places* (345) for the case of Mexican immigrants but does not elaborate.

20. Autor, "The Economics of Labor Market Intermediation"; Stovel and Shaw, "Brokerage."

21. Stovel and Shaw, "Brokerage," 147.

22. Autor, "The Economics of Labor Market Intermediation"; Williamson, *Markets and Hierarchy*.

23. This discussion of EAs focuses on how EAs are linked to the current literature on immigrant settlement rather than explaining the causes of EAs, as was done in chapter 2. This discussion also links EAs to the immigrant labor market outcomes.

24. Kasinitz and Rosenberg, "Missing the Connection"; W. Wilson, *The Truly Disadvantaged*; Mouw, "Are Black Workers Missing the Connection?"

25. W. Wilson, *The Truly Disadvantaged*.

26. New York City Department of City Planning, Chinatown Bus Study.

27. Sanders and Nee, "Limits of Ethnic Solidarity in the Enclave Economy."

28. K. Wilson and Portes, "Immigrant Enclaves"; Portes and Shafter, "Revisiting the Enclave Hypothesis"; Zhou, *Chinatown*.

29. Sanders and Nee, "Limits of Ethnic Solidarity in the Enclave Economy."

30. Kwong, *The Forbidden Workers*.

31. Zeng, "Difficult to Find Jobs."

32. Bailey and Waldinger, "Primary, Secondary, and Enclave Labor Markets."

33. Massey, *New Faces in New Places*. Massey's classification of states includes four categories. The first category is the Big Five: California, New York, Texas, Florida, and Illinois. The second category is the Second Tier: New Jersey, Massachusetts, Washington, Virginia, and Maryland. The third category is New Destination States, including twenty states such as Arizona and Colorado. The final category is Remaining States, those not included in the other three categories.

34. See Flippen and Kim, "Immigrant Context and Opportunity"; Waters and Jimenez, "Assessing Immigrant Assimilation."

35. See chapter 5 for discussion of employers' hiring preferences and practices.

36. Liu, Liang, and Chunyu, "Chinese Immigrant Entrepreneurs in the United States."

37. Liang et al., "From Chinatown to Everytown."

38. Brzozowski and Cucculelli, "Transnational Ties."

39. Economic historian Susan Carter documented historical evidence of Chinese immigrant settlement in non-gateway destinations ("Embracing Isolation"). Also see Chen, *Chop Suey*, for a systematic treatment of the historical development of Chinese restaurants in the United States. Although historically, there were some Chinese restaurants in small towns and faraway places in the country, today's dramatic expansion of Chinese restaurants is on a different scale (Jennifer 8. Lee, *The Fortune Cookie Chronicles*). Lee estimates there were some 40,000 Chinese restaurants in the United States, more than the number of McDonalds, Burger Kings, and KFCs combined. Of course, the expansion of Chinese restaurants is a global phenomenon as rising emigrants from China reach different parts of the world (see Roberts, *China to Chinatown*).

40. Sanders and Nee, "Limits of Ethnic Solidarity in the Enclave Economy"; Xie and Gough, "Ethnic Enclaves and the Earnings of Immigrants."

41. Fennelly, "Latinos, Africans, and Asians in the North Star State: Immigrant Communities in Minnesota"; Massey and Capoferro, "The Geographic Diversification of American Immigration"; Marrow, *New Destinations Dreaming*.

42. Bailey and Waldinger, "Primary, Secondary, and Enclave Labor Markets."

43. Bonacich and Modell, *The Economic Basis of Ethnic Solidarity*; Light, *Deflecting Immigration*; Portes, *The Economic Sociology of Immigration*; Portes and Rumbaut, *Immigrant America*.

44. Sassen, "Immigration and Local Labor Markets."

45. See Fong, Luk, and Ooka, "Spatial Distribution of Suburban Ethnic Businesses."

46. Fong, Luk, and Ooka, "Spatial Distribution of Suburban Ethnic Businesses."

CHAPTER 5. NEW BUSINESSES IN NEW PLACES

1. See Appendix A for more on the selection of these six states.

2. Fong, Luk, and Ooka, "Spatial Distribution of Suburban Ethnic Businesses."

3. Bonacich and Modell, *The Economic Basis of Ethnic Solidarity*; Portes, *Economic Sociology*.

4. Jennifer Lee, *Civility in the City*; Min, *Caught in the Middle*; Yoon, *On My Own*.

5. Jennifer Lee, *Civility in the City*; Jennifer Lee, "Constructing Race and Civility in Urban America"; Min, *Caught in the Middle*; Yoon, *On My Own*.

6. E. Anderson, *Streetwise*; Goffman, *On the Run*; Jennifer Lee, *Civility in the City*; Jennifer Lee, "Constructing Race and Civility in Urban America."

7. Massey, *New Faces in New Places*, 7.

8. I am grateful to one reviewer who helped clarify this point.

9. Bailey and Waldinger, "Primary, Secondary, and Enclave Labor Markets."

10. E. Wilson, "Bridging the Service Divide"; Zukin, *The Cultures of Cities*.

11. One reviewer asked about the relationship between Chinese immigrant entrepreneurs and African American employees. Our original research design focuses more on business owners' experiences of discrimination rather than hiring preferences and practices (except the use of EAs). I hope to explore this in future research.

12. Chinese business owners are not always clear about the country of origin of Spanish speaking workers. They tend to label them as "Mexicans" even though some may come from countries other than Mexico.

13. Dhingra, *Life Behind the Lobby.*

14. 1.5 generation refers to immigrants who came to the United States before or during their teens.

15. Fennelly, "Prejudice toward Immigrants in the Midwest."

16. Marrow, *New Destinations Dreaming.*

17. Marrow, "Immigrant Bureaucratic Incorporation."

18. Tropp et al., "How Contact Experiences Shape Welcoming."

19. Telles, Sawyer, and Rivera-Salgado, *Just Neighbors?*

20. Beck, *New York's Chinatown.* I thank one reviewer for making this suggestion.

21. Liu, *From Canton Restaurant to Panda Express.*

22. Liu, *From Canton Restaurant to Panda Express.*

23. Riccardi, "The Wonderful World of Louis Armstrong."

24. Weitzer, "Racial Prejudice Among Korean Merchants."

25. E. Anderson, *Streetwise.*

26. Jennifer Lee, *Civility in the City*; Jennifer Lee, "Constructing Race and Civility in Urban America."

27. Goffman, *On the Run.*

28. Min, *Caught in the Middle*; Yoon, *On My Own.*

29. Jennifer Lee, *Civility in the City.*

30. Jennifer Lee, *Civility in the City*; Jennifer Lee, "Constructing Race and Civility in Urban America."

31. Jennifer Lee, "Constructing Race and Civility in Urban America."

32. Jennifer Lee, "Constructing Race and Civility in Urban America."

33. Jennifer Lee, "Constructing Race and Civility in Urban America."

34. Guangzhou Daily, "Promoting 'Low Sodium Chinese Meals.'"

35. Foner and Dreby, "Relations Between the Generations in Immigrant Families."

36. See also Tropp et al., "How Contact Experiences Shape Welcoming."

37. BBC News, "Florida Shooting."

38. Shaw, "Chinese Immigrants in Philly Still Recovering from Home-Invasion Terror."

39. China News, "Chinese Restaurants Facing Challenges."

40. Tai, "Anti-Violence Rally in Philadelphia"; Associated Press, "Philadelphia Community Protests Crimes Against Chinese-Americans"; Xiao, "Refuse to Be Victims of Violence."

41. Min, *Caught in the Middle*; Yoon, *On My Own.*

42. Lee, "Constructing Race and Civility in Urban America," 916.

CHAPTER 6. THE TIES THAT BIND

1. Flippen and Farrell-Bryan, "New Destinations and Changing Geography of Immigrant Incorporation"; Hall, "Residential Integration"; Okamoto and Elbert, "Beyond Ballot Box."

2. Logan, Alba, and McNulty, "Ethnic Economies in Metropolitan Regions"; Massey and Denton, "Spatial Assimilation As Socioeconomic Outcome."

3. Massey and Denton, "Spatial Assimilation as Socioeconomic Outcome."

4. W. Li, "Anatomy of a New Ethnic Settlement."

5. Flippen and Farrell-Bryan, "New Destinations and Changing Geography of Immigrant Incorporation."

6. Levitt, *Transnational Villagers*.

7. The ease of international travel is referring to the situation before COVID-19.

8. Levitt, *Transnational Villagers*.

9. Lohnert and Steinbrink, "Rural and Urban Livelihoods."

10. Liang, Li, and Ma, "Migration and Remittances."

11. As noted earlier, Chinese immigrant entrepreneurs not only specialize in Chinese restaurants, but more recently are also likely to go into the Japanese restaurant business. It is fair to say that many of the Japanese restaurants that one sees in the United States are run by Chinese immigrants.

12. Liang et al., "Cumulative Causation."

13. DiPrete and Eirich, "Cumulative Advantage."

14. I have discussed the emergence of EAs and their functions earlier in the book. However, the discussion of EAs here mainly focuses on the economic ties between new destinations and Manhattan's Chinatown.

15. In addition to these economic linkages, many business owners mentioned that they also use accountants in New York City for tax returns each year.

16. Luo, "Immigrants Hear God's Word."

17. Luo, "Immigrants Hear God's Word."

18. Connor, "Religion as Resource"; Foner and Alba, "Immigrant Religion"; Hirschman, "The Role of Religion"; Guest, *God in Chinatown*; Min and Kim, *Religions in Asian America*; Yang, *Chinese Christians in America*.

19. Hirschman, "The Role of Religion."

20. Guest, *God in Chinatown.*

21. Luo, "Immigrants Hear God's Word."

22. Monday and Wednesday are often slow business days for restaurants.

23. This is the way they greet each other: "sisters and brothers" (*xiongdi jiemei*).

24. Turkle, *Alone Together.*

CHAPTER 7. CONCLUSION

1. Flippen and Farrell-Bryan, "New Destinations"; Hirschman and Massey, "Places and People."

2. Massey and Denton, "Spatial Assimilation."

3. Ruef, *The Entrepreneurial Group.*

4. Moritt, *The New Geography of Jobs.*

5. Jennifer 8. Lee, *The Fortune Cookie Chronicles.*

6. Liu, Liang, and Chunyu, "Chinese Immigrant Entrepreneurs."

7. Liu, Liang, and Chunyu, "Chinese Immigrant Entrepreneurs."

8. Sanders and Nee, "The Limits of Ethnic Solidarity"; Portes and Jenson, "The Enclave and the Entrants"; Zhou, *Chinatown.*

9. Massey, "Why Does Immigration Occur?"

10. This "win-win" story needs to be qualified as it only describes financial and economic mobility. However, money is not everything. This is especially the case for immigrant workers. For immigrant workers, working in new destinations often means that they have to endure social isolation away from the immigrant community and sometimes their families, as documented in chapter 6. This social isolation can also lead to mental health issues as well; see Liang and Zhou, "Legal Status and Labor Market and Health Consequences."

11. Hirschman, "Immigration and the American Century"; Jiménez, *The Other Side of Assimilation.*

12. Jiménez, *The Other Side of Assimilation.*

13. Liang and Zhou, "The Rise of Market-Based Job Search Institutions"; Hilgers, "The Kitchen Networks."

14. Jefferies, "The Amazing Chinatown Bus Network"; Klein, "Emergent Curbside Intercity Bus Industry."

15. Liang and Zhou, "Legal Status and Labor Market and Health Consequences"; Luo, "Immigrants Hear God's Word."

16. Overseas Chinese Daily, "12 Chinese Restaurants in Philadelphia Were Robbed at Gun Point."

17. Jennifer Lee, *Civility in the City*; Min, *Caught in the Middle*.

18. Hu, Tsui, and Guerrero, "Closing of Beloved Dim Sum Hall."

19. Yan, "88 Palace to Close."

20. Liang, "Spatial Diffusion of Low-skilled Chinese Immigrants in the Context of COVID-19."

21. Venkatranan, "String of Attacks."

22. Rothman and Feinberg, "An American Dream, Tarnished."

23. R. Lee, "The Decline of Chinatown in the United States," 432.

24. Tsui, "The End of Chinatown"; Campbell, "Suburbs: new Chinatowns."

25. Semuels, "The End of America's Chinatowns."

26. There may be three Chinatowns in New York City right now, one in Manhattan and the other two in Flushing, Queens, and Sunset Park, Brooklyn. There may be more Chinese immigrants who live in Flushing or Sunset Park. However, the rich culture and history associated with Manhattan's Chinatown, and its close linkages with new immigrant destinations in the United States, cannot be replaced. It should also be noted that international and domestic tourists often visit Manhattan's Chinatown and are unlikely to visit Chinatowns in Flushing or Sunset Park.

27. State of New York, "Governor Kathy Hochul Announces." Emphasis mine.

APPENDIX B: ANALYSIS OF JOB LOCATIONS

1. See http://www.fbi.gov/ucr/cius2007/data/table_10.html.

2. Long, *Regression Models for Categorical and Limited Dependent Variables*; Long and Freese, *Regression Models for Categorical Dependent Variables Using Stata*; Berk and MacDonald, "Overdispersion and Poisson Regression."

3. Berk and MacDonald, "Overdispersion and Poisson Regression," 13; Greene, *Econometric Analysis*, 744–45.

4. Long and Freese, *Regression Models for Categorical Dependent Variables Using Stata*, 372–73; Berk and MacDonald, "Overdispersion and Poisson Regression," 12–14.

5. Portes, *The Economic Sociology of Immigration*.

6. Card and Lewis, "The Diffusion of Mexican Immigrants during the 1990s: Explanations and Impacts."

7. Crowder and South, "Spatial Dynamics of White Flight."

8. Raudenbush and Bryk, *Hierarchical Linear Models*.

9. We estimated identical models using the 2010 survey data as well and obtained very similar results.

10. Anselin, *Spatial Econometrics*; Chi and Zhu, "Spatial Regression Models for Demographic Analysis."

11. Anselin, *Spatial Econometric.*

12. Chi and Zhu, "Spatial Regression Models for Demographic Analysis."

References

Alba, Richard, and Victor Nee. *Remaking the American Mainstream: Assimilation and Contemporary Immigration.* Cambridge, MA: Harvard University Press, 2003.

Anderson, Brett. "With Chop and Suey and Loyal Fans, a Montana Kitchen Keeps the Flame Burning." *The New York Times.* August 3, 2021. https://www.nytimes.com/2021/08/03/dining/pekin-noodle -parlor-butte-montana.html.

Anderson, Elijah. *Street Wise: Race, Class, and Change in an Urban Community.* Chicago: University of Chicago Press, 1990.

Anselin, Luc. *Spatial Econometrics: Methods and Models.* New York: Springer Science & Business Media, 1998.

Associated Press. "Philadelphia Community Protests Crimes Against Chinese-Americans." October 16, 2016. https://www.nbcphiladelphia .com/news/local/philadelphia-community-protests-crimes-against -chinese-americans/59778/.

Autor, David H. "The Economics of Labor Market Intermediation: An Analytic Framework." IZA Discussion Papers No. 3705, Institute for the Study of Labor (IZA), Bonn, 2008. http://nbn-resolving.de/urn: nbn:de:101:1-20081014429.

Bailey, Thomas, and Roger Waldinger. "Primary, Secondary, and Enclave Labor Markets: A Training System Approach." *American Sociological Review* 56, no. 4 (1991): 432–45.

Beck, Louis. *New York's Chinatown: A Historical Presentation of People and Places*. New York: Bohemia Publishing Company, 1892.

Berk, Richard, and John M. MacDonald. "Overdispersion and Poisson Regression." *Journal of Quantitative Criminology* 24, no. 3 (2008): 269–84.

BBC News. "Florida Shooting: West Point Admits Murdered Hero Peter Wang." February 21, 2018. Accessed January 12, 2021. https://www.bbc.com/news/world-us-canada-43132215.

Bonacich, E., and Suzanne Modell. *The Economic Basis of Ethnic Solidarity: Small Business in Japanese American Community*. Berkeley: University of California Press, 1980.

Boswell, Terry E. "A Split Labor Market Analysis of Discrimination against Chinese Immigrants, 1850-1882." *American Sociological Review* 51 (June 1986): 352–71.

Brzozowski, J., and M. Cucculelli. "Transnational Ties and Performance of Immigrant Firms: Evidence from Central Italy." *International Journal of Entrepreneurial Behavior & Research* 26 (2020): 1787–1806.

Campbell, Alexia Fernández. "Suburbs: The New Chinatowns." *The Atlantic*. May 18, 2016. https://www.theatlantic.com/business/archive/2016/05/suburbs-the-new-chinatowns/483375.

Cao, Jian. "Immigrants Face Difficult Times in Light of Increased Raids in Workplaces." *World Journal*, March 31, 2009, C1.

Card, David, and Ethan G. Lewis. "The Diffusion of Mexican Immigrants during the 1990s: Explanations and Impacts." In *Mexican Immigration to the United States*, edited by George J. Borjas, 193–228. Chicago: University of Chicago Press, 2005.

Carter, Susan B. "Embracing Isolation: Chinese American Geographic Redistribution During the Exclusion Era, 1882–1943." Paper presented at the Annual Meeting of the Population Association of America, San Francisco, CA, 2012.

Chaddick Institute of Metropolitan Development. *Adding on Amenities, Broadening the Base: 2014 Year in Review of Inter-city Bus Service in the United States*. DePaul University, 2015. https://las.depaul.edu/centers-and-institutes/chaddick-institute-for-metropolitan-development/research-and-publications/Documents/2014-Year-in-Review-of-Intercity-Bus-Service-in-the-United-States.pdf

Chen, Yong. *Chop Suey, USA: The Story of Chinese Food in America*. New York: Columbia University Press, 2015.

Chew, Kenneth S.Y., and John M. Liu. "Hidden in Plain Sight: Global Labor Force Exchange in the Chinese American Population, 1880–1940." *Population and Development Review* 30 (2004): 57–78.

Chi, Guangqing, and Jun Zhu. "Spatial Regression Models for Demographic Analysis." *Population Research and Policy Review* 27 (2008):17–42.

Chin, Ko-lin. *Smuggled Chinese: Clandestine Immigration to the United States*. Philadelphia, PA: Temple University Press, 2022.

China, Qiaowang. "Chinese Immigrants Lost Millions in Private Loan Associations." May 30, 2017. http://www.chinaqw.com/hqhr/2017/05 -30/144392.shtml.

"China Villa Envy: Emigration is Not Driven by Relative, No Absolute, Poverty." *The Economist*. May 13, 2004. https://www.economist.com /node/2677840/print?Story_ID=2677840.

China News. "世界日报：美华人拥枪自卫示威发声 扭转软弱形象" [Chinese Restaurants Facing Challenges of Crime and Robbery]. October 28, 2016. http://www.chinanews.com/m/hr/2016/10-28/8046468.shtml.

Chinatown Bus Stories Project (@chinatownbusstories). Instagram, accessed November 8, 2018. https://www.instagram.com/chinatown busstories/?hl=en/.

Connor, Philip. "Religion as Resource and Immigrant Economic Assimilation." *Social Science Research* 40, no. 5 (September 2011): 1350–61.

Crowder, Kyle, and Scott J. South. "Spatial Dynamics of White Flight: The Effects of Local and Extralocal Racial Conditions on Neighborhood Out-Migration." *American Sociological Review* 73, no. 5 (2008): 792–812.

Daniels, Roger. *Asian America: Chinese and Japanese in the United States Since 1850*. Seattle: University of Washington Press, 1988.

Diaz, Christina, and Peter D. Ore. "Landscapes of Appropriation and Assimilation: The Impact of Immigrant-Origin Populations on U.S. Cuisine." *Journal of Ethnic and Migration Studies*. Published ahead of print, September 09, 2020. https://doi.org/10.1080/1369183X.2020 .1811653.

DiPrete, Thomas, and Gregory M. Eirich. "Cumulative Advantage as a Mechanism for Inequality: A Review of Theoretical and Empirical Developments." *Annual Review of Sociology* 32 (2006): 271–97.

Dhingra, Pawan. *Life Behind the Lobby: Indian American Motel Owners and the American Dream*. Stanford, CA: Stanford University Press, 2012.

Dolnick, Sam. "Many Immigrants' Job Search Start in Chinatown." *The New York Times.* February 22, 2011. Accessed March 18, 2017. http://www.nytimes.com/2011/02/23/nyregion/23chinatown.html.

Donato, Katherine M., Charles Tolbert, Alfred Nucci, and Yukio Kawanno. "Changing Faces, Changing Places: The Emergence of New Non-Metropolitan Immigrant Gateways." In *New Faces in New Places: The Changing Geography of American* Immigration, edited by Douglas S. Massey, 75–98. New York: Russell Sage Foundation, 2008.

Eskebnazi, Marc Philippe, and Myles Kane. "Farewell, Fung Wah." *The New Yorker,* March 12, 2013. Accessed November 8, 2018. https://www.newyorker.com/humor/daily- shouts/farewell-fung-wah.

Fennelly, Katherine. "Latinos, Africans, and Asians in the North Star State: Immigrant Communities in Minnesota." In *Beyond the Gateway: Immigrants in A Changing America*, edited by Elizbeth M. Gozdziak and Susan F. Martin, 111–36. Lanham, MD: Lexington Books, 2005.

———. "Prejudice Toward Immigrants in the Midwest." In *New Faces in New Places: The Changing Geography of American Immigration*, edited by Douglas S. Massey, 151–78. New York: Russell Sage Foundation, 2008.

Flippen, Chenoa A., and Eunbi Kim. "Immigrant Context and Opportunity: New Destinations and Socioeconomic Attainment among Asians in the United States." *The Annals of the American Academy of Political and Social Science* 660 (July 2015): 175–98.

Flippen, Chenoa A., and Dylan Farrell-Bryan. 2021. "New Destinations and Changing Geography of Immigrant Incorporation." *Annual Review of Sociology* 47 (July 2021): 479–500.

Foner, Nancy. *From Ellis Island to JFK: New York's Two Great Waves of Immigration.* New Haven, CT: Yale University Press, 2000.

———, ed. *One Out of Three: Immigrant New York in the Twenty-First Century.* New York: Columbia University Press, 2013.

Foner, Nancy, and Richard Alba. "Immigrant Religion in the U.S. and Western Europe: Bridge or Barrier to Inclusion?" *International Migration Review* 42 (2008): 360–92.

Foner, Nancy, and Joanna Dreby. "Relations Between Generations in Immigrant Families." *Annual Review of Sociology* 37 (2011): 545–64.

Fong, Eric, Chiu Luk, and E. Ooka. "Spatial Distribution of Suburban Ethnic Businesses." *Social Science Research* 34, no. 1 (2005): 215–35.

Fuchs, Chris. "Fung Wah Bus Company Shut Down for Good." NBC News. July 17, 2015. https://www.nbcnews.com/news/asian-america/fung-wah-bus-company-closes-doors-good-n394026.

Geertz, Clifford. "The Rotating Credit Association: A 'Middle-Rung' in Development." *Economic Development and Cultural Change* 94 (1963): 241–63.

Goffman, Alice. *On the Run: Fugitive Life in An American City*. Chicago: The University of Chicago Press, 2014.

Gordon, Milton. *Assimilation in American Life: The Role of Race, Religion, and National Origins*. New York: Oxford University Press, 1964.

Gozdziak, Elzbieta M., and Susan Martin. *Beyond the Gateway: Immigrants in a Changing America*. New York: Lexington Books, 2005.

Granovetter, Mark. "The Economic Sociology of Firms and Entrepreneurs." In *The Economic Sociology of Immigration: Essays in Networks, Ethnicity and Entrepreneurship*, edited by Alejandro Portes, 128–65. New York: Russell Sage Foundation, 1995.

Guangzhou Daily. "美国费城提倡'低盐中餐'华人社团积极响应." [Promoting Low Sodium Chinese Meals]. *China News*, August 26, 2013. Accessed March 10, 2021. http://www.chinanews.com/hr/2013/08-26/5203956.shtml.

Guest, Kenneth J. *God In Chinatown: Religion and Survival in New York's Evolving Immigrant Community*. New York: New York University Press, 2003.

Hall, Mathew. "Residential Integration on the New Frontier: Immigrant Segregation in Established and New Destinations." *Demography* 50 (2013): 1873–96.

Hall, Mathew, and Kyle Crowder. "Native Out-Migration and Neighborhood Immigration in New Destinations." *Demography* 51 (2014): 2179–202.

Hilgers, Lauren. "The Kitchen Networks: America's Underground Chinese Restaurant Workers." *The New Yorker*, October 14, 2014. Accessed March 18, 2017. http://www.newyorker.com/magazine/2014/10/13/cooka%C2%80%C2%99s-tale.

———. *Patriot Number One: A Chinese Rebel Comes to America*. New York: Random House, 2018.

Hirschman, Charles. "The Role of Religion in the Origins and Adaptation of Immigrant Groups in the United States." *International Migration Review* 38 (2004): 1206–33.

———. "Immigration and the American Century." *Demography* 42 (2005): 595–620.

Hirschman, Charles, Philip Kasinitz, and Josh DeWind. *Handbook of International Migration: The American Experience*. New York: Russell Sage Foundation Press, 1999.

Hirschman, Charles, and Douglas S. Massey. "Places and People: The New American Mosaic." In *New Faces in New Places: The Changing Geography of American Immigration*, edited by Douglas S. Massey, 1–21. New York: Russell Sage Foundation, 2008.

Hooper, Kate, and Jeanne Batalova. "Chinese Immigrants in the United States." January 28, 2015. https://www.migrationpolicy.org/article/chinese-immigrants-united-states--2013.

Hsin, Amy, and Sofya Aptekar. "The Violence of Asylum: The Case of Chinese Undocumented Immigrants in the U.S." *Social Forces* 100 (2022): 1195–1217.

Hu, Winnie, Anjali Tsui, and Melissa Guerrero. "Closing of Beloved Dim Sum Hall Leaves a 'Crater' in Reeling Chinatown." *The New York Times*, March 10, 2021. https://www.nytimes.com/2021/03/10/nyregion/chinatown-restaurant-closures-coronavirus.html.

Huang, Pien. "Artists Pay Tribute to No-Frills Chinatown Bus, Discomforts and All." *National Public Radio*. March 29, 2016. https://www.npr.org/2016/03/29/472232857/defunct-chinatown-bus-line-celebrated-by-performers-ex-riders.

Hum, Tarry. *Making a Global Immigrant Neighborhood: Brooklyn's Sunset Park*. Philadelphia: Temple University Press, 2014.

Jefferies, Adrianne. "The Amazing Chinatown Bus Network." VICE, November 27, 2014. Accessed November 9, 2019. https://www.vice.com/en_us/article/qkve8m/down-to-chinatown.

Jiménez, Tomás R. *The Other Side of Assimilation*. Berkeley: University of California Press, 2017.

Jiménez, Tomás R., and Adam Horowitz. "When White is Just Alright: How Immigrants Redefine Achievement and Reconfigure the Ethnoracial Hierarchy." *American Sociological Review* 78, no.5: 849–71.

Kain, John F. "The Spatial Mismatch Hypothesis: Three Decades Later." *Housing Policy Debate* 3, no. 2 (1992): 371–92.

Kandel, William, and Emilio A. Parrado. "Restructuring of the US Meat Processing Industry and New Hispanic Migrant Destinations." *Population and Development Review* 31, no. 3 (2005): 447–71.

Kasinitz, Philip, and Jan Rosenberg. "Missing the Connection: Social Isolation and Employment on the Brooklyn Waterfront." *Social Problems* 43, no.2 (1996): 180–96.

Keefe, Patrick Radden. "The Snakehead." *The New Yorker*, April 16, 2006. https://www.newyorker.com/magazine/2006/04/24/the-snakehead.

Kinkead, Gwen. *Chinatown: A Portrait of a Closed Society*. New York: HarperCollins Publishers, 1992.

Klein, Nicholas J. "Emergent Curbside Intercity Bus Industry: Chinatown and Beyond." *Transportation Research Record: Journal of Transportation Research Board*, no. 2011 (2009): 83–89.

Klein, Nicholas, and Andrew Zitcer. "Everything But the Chickens: Cultural Authenticity on Board the Chinatown Bus." *Urban Geography* 33, no.1 (2012): 46–63.

Kwong, Peter. *The Forbidden Workers: Illegal Chinese Immigrants and American Labor*. New York: The New Press, 1997.

———. *The New Chinatown*. New York: Hill and Wang, 1996.

Kwong, Peter, and Dusanka Miscevic. *Chinese America: The Untold Story of America's Oldest New Community*. New York: The New Press, 2005.

Leach, Mark A., and Frank D. Bean. "The Structure and Dynamics of Mexican Migration to New Destinations in the United States." In *New Faces in New Places: The Changing Geography of American Immigration*, edited by Douglas S. Massey, 51–74. New York: Russell Sage Foundation, 2008.

Lee, Jennifer. *Civility in the City: Blacks, Jews and Koreans in Urban America*. Cambridge: Harvard University Press, 2002.

———. "Constructing Race and Civility in Urban America." *Urban Studies* 43, no. 5/6 (2006): 903–17.

Lee, Jennifer 8. *The Fortune Cookie Chronicles: Adventures in the World of Chinese Food*. New York: Hachette Book Group, 2009.

Lee, Rose Hum. "The Decline of Chinatown in the United States." *American Journal of Sociology* 54, no. 3 (1949): 422.

Levitt. Peggy. *Transnational Villagers*. Berkeley: University of California Press, 2001.

Li, Jingjin. "New Yorker Writer's Chinese Food Poem Sparks Racist Rucks." *Global Times*, April 13, 2016. https://www.globaltimes.cn/content/978405.shtml.

Li, Muqian. "The Closing of Some Chinatown Buses Hurt Small Businesses in Chinatown." *The World Journal*, March 3, 2013: C1.

Li, Wei. "Anatomy of a New Ethnic Settlement: the Chinese Ethnoburb in Los Angeles." *Urban Studies* 35, no. 3 (1998): 479–501.

———. "Los Angeles' Chinese Ethnoburb: From Ethnic Service Center to Global Economy Outpost." *Urban Geography* 19, no. 6 (2000): 502–17.

Liang, Zai. "Rules of the Game and Game of the Rules: The Politics of Recent Chinese Immigration to New York City." In *Migration,*

Transnationalism, and the Political Economy of New York, edited by Hector Cordero-Guzman, Ramon Grosfoguel, and Robert Smith, 131–45. Philadelphia, PA: Temple University Press, 2001.

———. "Demography of Illicit Emigration from China: A Sending Country's Perspective." *Sociological Forum* 16, no.4 (2001): 677–701.

———. "Spatial Diffusion of Low-skilled Chinese Immigrants in the Context of COVID-19." Paper presented at Annual Meeting of Eastern Sociological Society, February 18, 2021.

Liang, Zai, Miao David Chunyu, Guotu Zhuang, and Wenzhen Ye. "Cumulative Causation, Market Transition, and Emigration from China." *American Journal of Sociology* 114, no. 3 (2008): 706–37.

Liang, Zai, Jiejin Li, and Zhongdong Ma. "Migration and Remittances: Evidence from a Poor Province in China." *Asian Population Studies* 9, no. 2 (2013): 124–41.

Liang, Zai, Jiejin Li, Glenn Deane, Zhen Li, and Bo Zhou. "From Chinatown to Everytown: New Patterns of Employment for Low-Skilled Chinese Immigrants in the United States." *Social Forces* 97, no. 2 (2018): 893–919.

Liang, Zai, and Qian Jasmine Song. "Migration in China." In *International Handbook of Migration and Population Distribution*, edited by Michael J. White, 285–310. New York: Springer Handbook Series, 2016.

Liang, Zai, and Wenzhen Ye."From Fujian to New York: Understanding the New Chinese Immigration." In *Global Human Smuggling: Comparative Perspectives*, edited by David Kyle and Rey Koslowski, 187–215. Baltimore, MD: Johns Hopkins University Press, 2001.

Liang, Zai, and Bo Zhou. "Legal Status and Labor Market and Health Consequences for Low-skilled Chinese Immigrants in the U.S." The ANNALS of the American Academy of Political and Social Science 666, no. 1 (July 2016): 150–63. https://doi.org/10.1177/000271621 6650632.

———. "The Rise of Market-Based Job Search Institutions and Job Niches for Low-Skilled Chinese Immigrants." *RSF: The Russell Sage Foundation Journal of the Social Sciences* 4, no. 1 (2018): 78–95.

Lichter, Daniel, Domerico Parisi, Michael C. Taquino, and Steven Michael Grice. "Residential Segregation in New Hispanic Destinations: Cities, Suburbs, and Rural Communities Compared." *Social Science Research* 39, no.2 (2010): 215–30.

Light, Ivan. *Deflecting Immigration: Networks, Markets, and Regulation in Los Angles*. New York: Russell Sage Foundation, 2006.

Light, Ivan, and Edna Bonacich. *Immigrant Entrepreneurs: Koreans in Los Angeles*. Berkeley: University of California Press, 1988.

Light, Ivan, and Carolyn Rosenstein. "Expanding the Interaction Theory of Entrepreneurship." In *The Economic Sociology of Immigration: Essays on Networks, Ethnicity, and Entrepreneurship*, edited by Alejandro Portes, 166–212. New York: Russell Sage Foundation, 2005.

Light, Ivan, George Sabagh, Mehdi Bozorgmehr, and Claudia Der-Martirosian. "Beyond the Ethnic Enclave Economy." *Social Problems* 41, no. 1 (February 1994): 65–80.

Lii, Jane H. "Neighborhood Report: Chinatown; Chinatown Agencies Fined Over Job-Seekers' Fees." *The New York Times*, August 14, 1994. https://www.nytimes.com/1994/08/14/nyregion/neighborhood-report-chinatown-chinatown-agencies-fined-over-job-seekers-fees.html.

———. "The Chinese Menu Guys." *The New York Times*, July 28, 1996. https://www.nytimes.com/1996/07/28/nyregion/the-chinese-menu-guys.html.

Lin, Jan. *Reconstructing Chinatown: Ethnic Enclave, Global Change*. Minneapolis: University of Minnesota Press, 1998.

Ling, Huping. *Chinese St. Louis: From Enclave to Cultural Community*. Philadelphia, PA: Temple University Press, 2004.

Liu, Haiming. *From Canton Restaurant to Panda Express: A History of Chinese Food in the United States*. New Brunswick, NJ: Rutgers University Press, 2015.

Liu, Han, Zai Liang, and Miao David Chunyu. "Chinese Immigrant Entrepreneurs in the United States: New Temporal and Spatial Dimension." *Journal of Ethnic and Migration Studies* (November 2021). https://doi.org/10.1080/1369183X.2021.2007063.

Logan, John R., Richard Alba, and Thomas L. McNulty. "Ethnic Economies in Metropolitan Regions: Miami and Beyond." *Social Forces* 72, no. 3 (1994): 691–724.

Logan, John R., Richard Alba, and Wenquan Zhang. "Immigrant Enclaves and Ethnic Communities in New York and Los Angles." *American Sociological Review* 67, no. 2 (2002): 299–322.

Lohnert, B., and M. Steinbrink. "Rural and Urban Livelihoods: A Translocal Perspective in A South African Context." *South African Geographical Journal* 87, no. 2 (2005): 95–103.

Long, Scott. *Regression Models for Categorical and Limited Dependent Variables*. Thousand Oaks, CA: Sage Publications, 1997.

Long, Scott, and Jeremy Freese. *Regression Models for Categorical Dependent Variables Using Stata*. 2nd ed. College Station, TX: Stata Press, 2006.

Lowy, Joan, and Dan Stamm. "The End of the Chinatown Bus?" NBC Philadelphia, May 31, 2012. Accessed November 8, 2018. https://www.nbcphiladelphia.com/news/breaking/Chinatown-Bus-Closures-New-Century-155948325.html.

Loewen, James W. *The Mississippi Chinese, Between Black and White*. Long Grove, IL: Waveland Press, 1988.

Luo, Michael. "Immigrants Hear God's Word, in Chinese, by Conference Call." *The New York Times*, May 21, 2006. Accessed February 26, 2009. https://www.nytimes.com/2006/05/21/nyregion/immigrants-hear-gods-word-in-chinese-via-conference-call.html.

———. "In Chinatown, a $10 Trip Means War; Weary Owners Struggle to Stay Afloat in Cutthroat Competition." *The New York Times*. February 2, 2004. https://www.nytimes.com/2004/02/21/nyregion/chinatown-10-trip-means-war-weary-owners-struggle-stay-afloat-cutthroat.html.

Marrow, Helen. "Immigrant Bureaucratic Incorporation: The Dual Roles of Professional Missions and Government Policies." *American Sociological Review* 74 (2009): 756–76.

———. *New Destinations Dreaming: Immigration, Race, and Legal Status in the Rural American South*. Stanford, CA: Stanford University Press, 2011.

Martinez, Jose. "Illegal Dollar-Van Drivers Hoping for the Light at the End of Pandemic Tunnel." *The City*. December 20, 2020. https://www.thecity.nyc/transportation/2020/12/15/22175385/nyc-dollar-van-drivers-suffering-during-pandemic.

Massey, Douglas S. "Why Does Immigration Occur?" In *The Handbook of International Migration: The American Experience*, edited by Charles Hirschman, Philip Kasinitz, and Josh DeWind, 34–52. New York: Russell Sage Foundation, 1999.

———. "The New Immigration and the Meaning of Ethnicity in the United States." *Population and Development Review* 21 (1995): 631–52.

Massey, Douglas S., ed. *New Faces in New Places: The Changing Geography of American Immigration*. New York: Russell Sage Foundation, 2008.

Massey, Douglas S., and Chiara Capoferro. "The Geographic Diversification of American Immigration." In *New Faces in New Places: The*

Changing Geography of American Immigration, edited by Douglas S. Massey, 25–50. New York: Russell Sage Foundation, 2008.

Massey, Douglas S., and Nancy Denton. "Spatial Assimilation as Socio-economic Outcome." *American Sociological Review* 50, no. 1 (1985): 94–106.

Mendelson, Anne. *Chow Chop Suey: Food and the Chinese American Journey*. New York: Columbia University Press, 2016.

Meyer, J.R., C.R. Oster, J.A. Gomez-Ibanez, and M. Clippinger. *Deregulation and the Future of Intercity Passenger Travel*. Cambridge: MIT Press, 1987.

Migration Policy Institute. *Immigrants from Asia in the United States*. March 10, 2021. https://www.migrationpolicy.org/article/immigrants-asia-united-states-2020#:~:text=In%20the%202014%2D18%20period,estimated%2011%20million%20unauthorized%20immigrants.

Min, Pyong Gap. *Caught in the Middle: Korean Merchants in America's Multiethnic Cities*. Berkeley: University of California Press, 1996.

———. "Settlement Patterns and Diversity." In *Asian Americans: Contemporary Trends and Issues*, 2nd ed, edited by Pyong Gap Min, 32–53. Thousand Oaks, CA: Pine Forge Press, 2005.

———. *Ethnic Solidarity for Economic Survival: Korean Greengrocers in New York City*. New York: Russell Sage Foundation, 2008.

Min, Pyong Gap, and Jung Ha Kim. *Religions in Asian America*. New York: AltaMira Press, 2002.

Moritt, Enrico. *The New Geography of Jobs*. New York: Mariner Books, 2012.

Mouw, Ted. "Are Black Workers Missing the Connection? The Effect of Spatial Distance and Employee Referrals on Interfirm Racial Segregation." *Demography* 39, no.3 (2002): 507–28.

National Academy of Sciences. *Economic and Fiscal Impact of Immigration*. National Academy of Science Press. 2017. https://www.nationalacademies.org/our-work/economic-and-fiscal-impact-of-immigration.

Nee, Victor, and Brett de Bary Nee. *Longtime Californ': Documentary Study of an American Chinatown*. New York, Pantheon Book, 1973.

Nee, Victor, Jimmy M. Sanders, and Scott Sernau. "Job Transitions in an Immigrant Metropolis: Ethnic Boundaries and the Mixed Economy." *American Sociological Review* 59, no. 6 (1994): 840–72.

New York City Department of City Planning. *Chinatown Bus Study*. 2009. http://www.nyc.gov/html/mancb3/downloads/cb3docs/chinatown_final_report.pdf.

Newman, Barry. "On the East Coast, Chinese Buses Give Greyhound a Run." *Wall Street Journal*, January 25, 2005: A1.

Office of Immigration Statistics. *2007 Yearbook of Immigration Statistics*. Washington, DC: U.S. Department of Homeland Security, 2008.

———. *2015 Yearbook of Immigration Statistics*. Washington, DC: U.S. Department of Homeland Security, 2016.

———. *2008 Yearbook of Immigration Statistics*. Washington, DC: U.S. Department of Homeland Security Office of Immigration Statistics, 2009.

Okamoto, Dina, and Kim Elbert. "Beyond Ballot Box: Immigrant Collective Action in Gateways and New Destinations." *Social Problems* 57, no. 4 (2010): 529–58.

Orum, Anthony M. "Circles of Influence and Chains of Command." *Social Forces* 84, no. 2 (2005): 921–39.

Overseas Chinese Daily. "费城暴发12起针对华人餐馆的抢劫 警民齐聚华埠商讨对策" [12 Chinese Restaurants in Philadelphia Were Robbed at Gun Point]. August 9, 2016. Accessed March 18, 2017. http://forums.huaren4us.com/archiver/showtopic.aspx?topicid=2051423.

Owen, Erika. "Anyone Who Has Ridden or Heard of the Chinatown Bus Will Love This Blog." December 27, 2016. https://www.travelandleisure.com/travel-tips/ground-transportation/chinatown-bus-stories-blog.

Park, Robert, and Earnest Burges. *Introduction to the Science of Sociology*. Chicago: The University of Chicago Press, 1924.

Parrado, Emile, and William Kandel. 2008. "New Hispanic Migrant Destinations: A Tale of Two Industries." In *New Faces in New Places: The Changing Geography of American Immigration*, edited by Douglas S. Massey, 99–123. New York: Russell Sage Foundation, 2008.

Portes, Alejandro. *Economic Sociology: A Systematic Inquiry*. Princeton, NJ: Princeton University Press, 2010.

———, ed. *The Economic Sociology of Immigration: Essays on Networks, Ethnicity, and Entrepreneurship*. New York: Russell Sage Foundation, 1995.

Portes, Alejandro, and Robert Bach. *Latin Journey*. Berkeley: University of California Press, 1985.

Portes, Alejandro, and Leif Jenson. "The Enclave and the Entrants: Patterns of Ethnic Enterprise in Miami before and after Mariel." *American Sociological Review* 54, no.6 (1989): 929–49.

Portes, Alejandro, and Ruben Rumbaut. *Immigrant America: A Portrait*. Berkeley: University of California Press, 2006.

Portes, Alejandro, and Julia Sensenbrenner. "Embeddedness and Immigration: Notes on the Social Determinants of Economic Action." *American Journal of Sociology* 98, no. 6 (1993): 1320–50.

Portes, Alejandro, and Steven Shafter. "Revisiting the Enclave Hypothesis: Miami Twenty-Five Years Later." *The Sociology of Entrepreneurship* 25 (2004): 157–90.

Portes, Alejandro and Min Zhou. "The New Second Generation: Segmented Assimilation amd Its Variants." *Annals of American Academy of Political and Social Science* 530 (1993): 74–96.

Ramsy, Austin. "Calvin Trillin's Poem on Chinese Food Proves Unpalatable for Some." *The New York Times*. April 7, 2016. https://www.nytimes .com/2016/04/08/world/asia/calvin-trillin-chinese-food-poem.html.

Raudenbush, Stephen W., and Anthony S. Bryk. *Hierarchical Linear Models: Applications and Data Analysis Methods*. Thousand Oaks, CA: Sage Publications, 2002.

Reiss, Aaron. "New York's Shadow Transit." *The New Yorker*. June 27, 2014. Accessed October 8, 2021. https://projects.newyorker.com/story /nyc-dollar-vans.

Riccardi, Ricky. "The Wonderful World of Louis Armstrong." February 31, 2011. Accessed February 18, 2021. https://dippermouth.blogspot.com /2011/02/cornet-chop-suey.html.

Roberts, J.A.G. *China to Chinatown: Chinese Food in the West*. Chicago, IL: University of Chicago Press, 2004.

Rothman, Julia, and Shanina Ferinberg. "An American Dream, Tarnished." *The New York Times*. February 25, 2021. https://www.nytimes .com/2021/02/25/business/covid-asian-american-attacks.html.

Ruef, Martin. *The Entrepreneurial Group: Social Identities, Relations, and Collective Action*. Princeton, NJ: Princeton University Press, 2010.

Sanders, Jimmy, and Victor Nee. "Limits of Ethnic Solidarity in the Enclave Economy." *American Sociological Review* 52, no. 6 (1987): 745–67.

Sassen, Saskia. "Immigration and Local Labor Markets." In *The Economic Sociology of Immigration: Essays on Networks, Ethnicity, and Entrepreneurship*, edited by Alejandro Portes, 87–127. New York: Russell Sage Foundation, 1995.

Schwieterman, Joseph P., Brian Antolin, Alexander Levin, Matthew Michel, and Heather Spray. "The Remaking of the Motor Coach: 2015 in Review of Intercity Bus Service in the United States." Chaddick Institute of Metropolitan Development at DePaul University, 2006. https://las.depaul.edu/centers-and-institutes/chaddick-institute-for

-metropolitan-development/research-and-publications/Documents /2015%20Year%20in%20Review%20of%20Intercity%20Bus%20 Service%20in%20the%20United%20States.pdf

Scott, Allen John. *Metropolis from the Division of Labor to Urban Form.* Berkeley: University of California Press, 1988.

Semuels, Alana. "The End of America's Chinatowns." *The Atlantic,* February 4, 2019. Accessed August 20, 2019. https://www.theatlantic .com/technology/archive/2019/02/americas-chinatowns-are -disappearing/581767.

Shaw, Julie. "Chinese Immigrants in Philly Still Recovering from Home-Invasion Terror." *The Philadelphia Inquirer.* October 6, 2017. Accessed October 20, 2019. https://www.philly.com/philly/news/crime/norman -bowen-anthony-campbell-chinese-takeout-owner-robberies-2017 1006.html.

Shah, Neil. "Immigrants from China Top those from Mexico." *The Wall Street Journal,* May 3, 2015. https://www.wsj.com/articles/immigrants -to-u-s-from-china-top-those-from-mexico-1430699284.

Singer, Audrey. *The Rise of New Immigrant Gateways.* Washington, DC: Center on Urban and Metropolitan Policy, The Brookings Institution, 2004.

State of New York. "Governor Kathy Hochul Announces Chinatown as $20 Million New York City Region Winner of Fifth Round Downtown Revitalization Initiative." November 10, 2021. https://www.governor.ny .gov/news/governor-hochul-announces-chinatown-20-million-new -york-city-region-winner-fifth-round.

Stovel, Katherine, and Lynette Shaw. "Brokerage." *Annual Review of Sociology* 38 (2012): 139–58.

Summathi, Reddy. "Illegal but Very Popular." *The Wall Street Journal.* September 13, 2012. https://www.wsj.com/articles/SB1000087239639 04447090045776500131399444418.

Sung, Betty Lee. *The Mountain of Gold: The Story of Chinese in America.* New York: Macmillan, 1967.

Tai, Sai. "Anti-Violence Rally in Philadelphia." *The China Press,* October 16, 2016. Accessed November 22, 2019. http://ny.uschinapress .com/m/spotlight/2016/10-16/105189.html.

Telles, Edward, Mark Q. Sawyer, and Gaspar Rivera-Salgado. *Just Neighbors?* New York: The Russell Sage Foundation Press, 2011.

Thomas, W. I., and Florian Znaniecki. *The Polish Peasant in Europe and America.* Urbana: University of Illinois Press, 1996.

Trillin, Calvin. "Have They Run out of Provinces Yet." *The New Yorker*, April 4, 2016. https://www.newyorker.com/magazine/2016/04/04/have-they-run-out-of-provinces-yet-by-calvin-trillin.

Tropp, Linda R., Dina G. Okamoto, Helen B. Marrow, and Michael Jones-Correa. "How Contact Experiences Shape Welcoming: Perspectives from U.S.-Born and Immigrant Groups." *Social Psychology Quarterly* 8 (2018): 23–47.

Tsui, Bonnie. "The End of Chinatown: Does China's Rise Mean the End of One of America's Most Storied Ethnic Enclaves?" *The Atlantic*, December, 2011. Accessed August 20, 2019. https://www.theatlantic.com/magazine/archive/2011/12/the-end-of-chinatown/308732.

———. *American Chinatown*. New York: Free Press, 2009.

Turkle, Sherry. *Alone Together: Why We Expect More from Technology and Less from Each Other*. New York: Basic Books, 2011.

US Census Bureau. "Tabulations from the 2013 American Community Survey." Table S0101. https://data.census.gov/cedsci/table?q=american%20community%20survey&tid=ACSST1Y2013.S0101.

Ungerleider, Neal. "Business Lessons from Chinatown Buses." *Fast Company*. June 5, 2012. https://www.fastcompany.com/1839333/business-lessons-chinatown-buses.

Venkatraman, Sakshi. "String of Attacks Against Older Asians Leaves Chinatowns in Big Cities on Edge." NBC News. February 29, 2021. https://www.nbcnews.com/news/asian-america/string-attacks-against-older-asians-leaves-big-city-chinatowns-edge-n1257157.

Waldinger, Roger. *Still the Promised City?: African Americans and New Immigrants in Post Industrial New York*. Cambridge, MA: Harvard University Press, 1996.

———. *Through the Eye of the Needle: Immigrants and Enterprise in New York's Garment Trades*. New York: New York University Press, 1986.

Wang, Hansi Lo. "Leaving China's North, Immigrants Redefine Chinese in New York." *National Public Radio*, January 16, 2016. https://www.npr.org/transcripts/463857599.

Waters, Mary, and Tomas R. Jimenez. "Assessing Immigrant Assimilation: New Empirical and Theoretical Challenges." *Annual Review of Sociology* 31 (2005): 105–25.

Weitzer, Ronald. "Racial Prejudice Among Korean Merchants in African American Neighborhoods." *The Sociological Quarterly* 38, no. 4 (1997): 587–606.

Williamson, Oliver. *Markets and Hierarchy: Analysis and Antitrust Implications*. New York: Free Press, 1975.

Wilson, Eli R. "Bridging the Service Divide: Dual Labor Niches and Embedded Opportunities in Restaurant Work." *RSF: The Russell Sage Foundation Journal of the Social Sciences* 4, no. 1 (2018): 115–27.

Wilson, Kenneth, and Alejandro Portes. "Immigrant Enclaves: An Analysis of the Labor Market Experiences of Cuban in Miami." *American Journal of Sociology* 86, no. 2 (1980): 295–319.

Wilson, William Julius. *The Truly Disadvantaged: The Inner City, the Underclass and Public Policy*. Chicago: University of Chicago, 1987.

Xiao, Xu. "人人持枪！不做哑裔！华人携枪大游行，警车开道护航 威武！" [Refuse to Be Victims of Violence, Chinese Immigrants in Philly Held Protest]. *The Atlanta*, 2016. Accessed October 16, 2019. http://www.atlanta168.com/p/201610/20161018/1_36880.html.

Xie, Yu, and Margret Gough. "Ethnic Enclaves and the Earnings of Immigrants." *Demography* 48, no. 4 (2011): 1293–315.

Xu, Yajun. "Council Woman Margret Chin and DOT Explain Bus Permit." *The World Journal*, July 27, 2013: C3.

Yan, Jiaying. "88 Palace to Close." *The World Journal*, September 23, 2020. Accessed August 15, 2021. https://www.worldjournal.com/wj/story/121382/4881829.

Yang, Fenggang. *Chinese Christians in America: Conversion, Assimilation, and Adhesive Identities*. University Park, PA: Pennsylvania State University Press, 1999.

Yoon, In-jin. *On My Own: Korean Businesses and Race Relations in America*. Chicago: University of Chicago Press, 1997.

Zeng, Huiyan. "Difficult to Find Jobs in Chinese Community in Times of Financial Crisis." *World Journal Magazine*, February 22, 2009: 16–20.

Zhou, Min. *Chinatown: The Socioeconomic Potential of an Urban Enclave*. Philadelphia, PA: Temple University Press, 1992.

———. "Diverse Origins and Destinies." In *One Out of Three: Immigrant New York in the Twenty-First Century*, edited by Nancy Foner, 120–47. New York: Columbia University Press, 2013.

Zhou, Yu. "Beyond Ethnic Enclaves: Location Strategies of Chinese Producer Service Firms in Los Angeles." *Economic Geography* 74, no. 3 (1998): 228–51.

Zhou, Yuting. "Hillary Clinton Hosting Fund-Raising Dinner in China-town." *The World Journal*, April 4, 2007: E2.

Zukin, Sharon. *The Cultures of Cities*. New York: Blackwell, 1995.

Zuniga, Victor, and Ruben Hernandez-Leon. *New Destinations: Mexican Immigration in the United States*. New York: Russell Sage Foundation, 2005.

Index

88 Palace, closing of, 141

African Americans, 46, 97–98, 163–64n14; connection of with Chinese food, 100; history of conflicts with minority merchants doing business in African American neighborhoods, 85–86, 168n11; models characterizing the relationship between immigrant business owners and black residents, 109–10
Alba, Richard, 50
American Civil Liberties Union (ACLU), 109
American Community Survey (ACS [2002–2017]), 4–5, 27, 28, 78
Armstrong, Louis, 100
Asian Americans, 50, 51
assimilation theory, 49–50; revised version of, 52–53; segmented assimilation, 164n19; spatial assimilation, 6–7

Bailey, Thomas, 82, 91
Beck, Louis, 100

Black Lives Matter (BLM) movement, 106
BoltBus, 52
Boston, 44, 46, ,47, 52, 57, 138, 143
Boswell, Terry E., 10
Bowery, the, 18
Brian, 33–34
Brooklyn, New York, 125, 126; Chinatown in, 160n1; Sunset park area of, 144, 145, 161n7
business owners (immigrant), 90, 98; descriptive statistics of business owners, 88*tab.*; Jewish business owners, 103; Korean business owners, 103, 110, 111; lack of legal immigration status by Chinese business owners, 111; and the "Matthew effect," 118; models characterizing the relationship between immigrant business owners and black residents, 109–10; mom-and-pop operations, 136; role of children in reducing tensions, 104–5; and social contact with local residents, 105–6; and the tense relationship between owners and customers and

193

business owners (immigrant) (*continued*)
ways to reduce tension, 103–4; three
categories of, 74–76; violence against
Chinese business owners, 108–9

Capoferro, Chiara, 5
Carter, Susan, 167n39
chefs (Chinese restaurant), and the
economic benefits debate, 67–68
Chen, 90–91, 102, 103
Chen, Guan, 1–2, 3
Chen, Kenneth, 74
Chen, Tim, 120–21, 123; as a devoted
Christian, 121; main business strategy
of, 121
Chen, Willington, 56–57, 140–41, 146
Chicago school of sociology, 49–50
China, 9*map.*
Chinatown, New York City (Manhattan), 4,
17*map.*, 18*map.*, 35, 112, 133, 137,
146–47, 163n6; changes in population
in two Chinatowns in New York City,
144*fig.*; decline in Manhattan's Chinatown population (2000–2010),
144–46; the end of Chinatown in Manhattan, 142–43; impact of COVID-19
on, 140–42; linkage to other Chinatowns, 57; population decline in,
56–57; and the printing of Chinese
menus, 116–19; spatial distribution of
shops related to the restaurant business in Chinatown, 116–18, 117*fig.*;
support of New York State for, 146–47;
three different Chinatowns in New
York City, 172n26; two parts of, 18
Chinatown buses/bus lines, 11, 21, 24,
38–39, 51–52, 59, 64–68, 124, 129, 138;
birth of the Chinatown bus industry,
40; Chinatown bus routes between
New York City and destination cities,
43*map.*; cutthroat competition among
Chinatown bus companies, 53–54;
development of, 53, 55–57; distribution
of bus routes by destination states,
42*tab.*; distribution of daily bus routes
by bus company, 41*tab.*; DOT crackdown on, 53–54; financial investment
in, 56; the Fung Wah bus (the first
Chinatown bus), 39, 44, 46–47, 57–58;

inception of in Fujian, 45–46; innovation of curbside buses, 39, 52–53; large
scale of, 44; and mainline bus compa-
nies, 138–39; passenger comments
concerning, 164–65n36; recent developments in, 79–80; spatial dispersion
of Chinese immigrants and Chinatown
buses, 44–49; spatial patterns of, 40
"Chinatown Bus Stories," 58
Chinatowns (various, in the United
States), 16, 112, 143; characteristics of
Chinese immigrants in, 16–17
Chinese Immigrant Associations (New
York and Philadelphia), 109
Chinese immigrant-owned business:
diffusion of, 7, 35–36; expansion of, 36
Chinese Restaurant News, 74
Chinese restaurants, 96; Chinese restaurants owners, 76; expansion of into
vast areas of the United States, 83;
hierarchy within, 34–35; location of
restaurants jobs, 73–74; number and
various spatial locations of, 2–3, 35*fig.*,
46; three types of workers in (Chinese
immigrants, Latinos, whites), 92–93;
unpleasant situations faced by, 102–3
Chinese Rifle Association in Greater
Philadelphia (CRAGP), 109
Christianity, 128
Chu, Jon, 56
church, as an institution helping immigrants integrate into a local community, 96–97, 98. *See also* religion,
practicing of in new immigrant
destinations
Church of Grace to Fujianese, 127–29, 131,
132
Community Policing, 108
Corpus Christi, Texas, 100
COVID-19 pandemic, 122, 163n6; impact
of on Chinatown, 140–42
credit rotation associations, 63, 166n12
Cuomo, Andrew, 54

Dayton, Ohio, 99
deunionization, of the workforce, 6
Diaz, Christina, 50
diversity index for Chinese immigrant
restaurant workers, 4–5

Dominican Republic, 114
DoorDash, 141

East Broadway, as "Fuzhou Street," 19
Eastern Bus Company, 49
economic ties, between New York City
    and new immigrant destinations,
    115–25; and the use of employment
    agencies, 123–24
Electronic Logging Device (ELD), 54
employment agencies (EAs), 3, 9, 10, 16,
    31–32, 64–68, 123–24, 146, 161n5,
    170n14; challenges faced by, 36–37;
    critical function of, 26–27; density of
    and locations in New York City, 19–20,
    20*fig.*, 21*fig.*; emergence of in New
    York City, 18–19; function of, 32; need
    of to attract Latino workers, 82;
    typical encounters between EA staff
    members and job applicants, 21–22.
    See also employment agencies (EAs),
    in Chinatown; employment agencies
    (EAs), two driving forces of
employment agencies (EAs), in China-
    town, 20*fig.*, 22, 61, 65–67, 91–92;
    Mr. Yang's employment agency,
    22–25; Wendy Wong's Sincere
    Employment Agency, 25–27
employment agencies (EAs), two driving
    forces of: increasing diversity of
    Chinese immigrants, 27–31
entrepreneurship, 51–52, 55–56, 79, 91,
    137, 168n11; challenges of in places
    like Texas and Florida that lack
    Chinese immigrant workers, 91–92; in
    immigrant enclaves ("ethnic enclaves")
    such as New York's Chinatown, Los
    Angeles's Koreatown, and Miami's
    Little Havana, 84, 137; and Japanese
    restaurants run by Chinese immi-
    grants, 170n11; and the logic of
    Chinese immigrant entrepreneurship,
    110; and socio-economic mobility,
    136–37; spatial diffusion/dispersion of
    Chinese immigrant entrepreneurs,
    31–36, 135–36, 163–64n14; survey of
    immigrant entrepreneurs in six states
    (Pennsylvania, Virginia, North Caro-
    lina, Florida, Ohio, and Texas), 84–86,

85*fig.*, 86; translocal immigrant entre-
    preneurs, 114–15; and the "win-win"
    situation for entrepreneurs, 81–82,
    137, 171n10
Eskebnazi, Marc-Philippe, 57
ethnic economies, 63

Farrell-Bryan, Dylan, 113, 114–15
Flippen, Chenoa A., 6, 61, 113, 114
Florida, 11, 84–86, 85*fig.*, 86, 91
Fong, Eric, 64, 83
Fujian province, China (immigrants
    from), 8, 18, 30–31, 45, 62, 65, 160n4;
    and Christianity, 128; and the incep-
    tion of Chinatown buses, 45–49
Fukien American Association, 8

gentrification, 143
Georgia, 46
Goffman, Alice, 89, 101
Golden Venture, ill-fated 1993 voyage of, 45
"good workers/good jobs," 23–24, 161n13
Gordon, Milton, 49–50
Greyhound Bus Lines, 25–26, 27, 48, 49, 52
Guangdong (Canton) province, 8, 18, 27,
    30, 31

Hirschman, Charles, 50, 128
Hispanics, 50, 97–98
Hochul, Kathy, 146, 147
hometown associations (HAs), Chinese,
    28–30, 162n24; distribution of in the
    United States, 29*tab.*; number of HAs
    of selected Chinese provinces in the
    United States, 30*tab.*
Horowitz, Adam, 51
Huang (Pastor Huang), 132–33

immigrants, 2, 3, 6–7, 10–11, 171n10;
    assimilation of individual immigrants
    to the assimilation of entrepre-
    neurs, 49–54, 138; challenges faced by,
    139–40; definition of, 161–62n16; geo-
    graphic diversification among recent
    immigrants, 6; immigrant settlement
    patterns, 113; in new destinations, 5.
    See also church, as an institution help-
    ing immigrants integrate into a local
    community; immigrants, new

immigrants (*continued*)
destinations for; *specifically listed individual immigrants*
immigrants, Asian and East Asian, 4, 143
immigrants, Chinese, 9, 30–31, 48, 104, 110, 127, 159n3; and the employment patterns of low-skilled Chinese immigrant workers, 9, 79–80, 80–81; low-skilled Chinese immigrants, 2, 3–4, 5, 6, 8, 10–11, 15, 19, 25, 26, 36, 46, 58, 83; in New York City, 62; and the spatial dispersion of Chinese immigrants and Chinatown buses, 44–49. *See also* spatial dispersion, of Chinese immigrants, theoretical implications of
immigrants, new destination choices for, 60–62; adapting to new destinations, 94–97; doing business in new immigrant destinations, 89–94; and new patterns of business expansion in new immigrant destination, 79–80; and the role of employment agencies, immigrant workers, and Chinatown buses, 64–68; shift to non-gateway destinations, 81–82, 167n39; socio-demographic characteristics of new immigrant destinations, 86, 87*fig.* *See also* race relations, in new destinations
immigrants, European, 50
immigrants, Irish, 10, 50
immigrants, Italian, 10, 50
immigrants, Jewish, 50
immigrants, Latino, 61, 92, 97
immigrants, Mexican, 4, 61, 124, 166n19
immigration: of the Chinese to the United States, 2, 27, 30–31; economic sociology of, 72, 82–83; literature concerning, 58–59
Immigration and Customs Enforcement (ICE), 33, 79
Immigration Reform and Control Act (IRCA [1986]), 5–6, 95
International Employment Agency, 47–48

Japanese restaurants, 170n11
Jay, 73
Jennifer, 73
Jiménez, Tomás, 50–51, 138

Jinfeng Restaurant, 141
JL bus company, 54
job searches, transition from network-based job searches to market-based job searches, 19–22
John, 106–7; cultural brokerage of, 107
Jonathan, 126–27

Kim, Enubi, 6, 61

Lee, Jackson, 25, 101
Lee, Jennifer, 103
Lee, Jennifer 8, 136, 167n39
Levitt, Peggy, 114
Li, James, 121–23
Li, Wei, 113
Liang, Peter Peiling, 44, 46–47, 57
Ling, Huping, 4
Liu, Haiming, 100
Liu, Han, 79, 95–96
Locke, Gary, 56
Loewen, James, 4
Los Angeles, 20, 34, 63, 64, 92, 124, 134
Lucky Dragon bus line, 47
Luk, Chiu, 64, 83

Malaysia, 45
Massey, Douglas S., 5, 71, 90, 166n19, 167n33
Megabus, 52–53
Mexicans/Mexican Americans, 92–93, 100. *See also* immigrants, Mexican
migration, 4
Min, Pyong Gap, 89, 109
Mississippi, Chinese immigrants in, 4
money, pooling of, 73
Mr. Jiang, 75
Mr. Yong Zheng, 93–94
Mr. Zhang, 91, 124, 125
Mr. Zheng, 74, 76
Ms. Huang, 47–48
Ms. Lin, 131–32
Ms. Song, 103–4
Ms. Wang, 105–8, 110

Nee, Victor, 50, 67
New York City, 89, 98–99, 137; rotation credit practices and financial losses of the Chinese community in, 63, 166n12; saturation of Chinese

restaurants in, 7–8, 62. *See also* Chinatown, New York City; economic ties,
between New York and new immigrant
destinations
North Carolina, 11, 46, 84–86, 85*fig.*, 86,
92; race relations in, 97–98

Ohio, 11, 46, 84–86, 85*fig.*, 86
Ooka, E., 64, 83
Ore, Peter D., 50
Orum, Anthony M., 50

Pennsylvania, 11, 84–86, 85*fig.*, 86
Peter, 106
Philadelphia, 84–86, 85*fig.*, 86, 89, 100,
110, 132–33, 138; anti-violence rally
in, 109*fig.*; business owners in northern Philadelphia, 100–102; high crime
rates in northern Philadelphia, 108
Portes, Alejandro, 10, 50, 67
Proposition 187 (California [1994]), 6,
159–60n9

race relations, in new destinations,
97–108; between Hispanics and
African Americans in North Carolina,
97–98; comparison between the context of race relations in New York City
and new destinations, 98–99; and
intimidation by white workers of
Chinese immigrants, 99; neighborhoods included in the study of,
99–100; race relations between
Korean merchants and black residents
in Washington, DC, 100
religion, practicing of in new immigrant
destinations, 127–33
Riccardi, Ricky, 100

Sanders, Jimmy, 67
San Francisco, 2, 60, 134, 137, 142, 143
Schumer, Chuck, 145
Singapore, 45
"snakehead smugglers," 45
social connections, between new York City
and new immigrant destinations,
125–27
social integration, through children's
cultural brokerage, 110–11
social isolation, 171n10

social media, 5, 11, 125, 129, 132, 133, 151
socio-economic mobility, 136–37
South Africa, 114
spatial assimilation, 6–7
spatial diffusion, 55, 89–90
spatial dispersion: of Chinese immigrants
and Chinatown buses, 44–49; of
Chinese immigrants, theoretical
implications of, 135–39
spatial distance, and the salary of chefs, 68
spatial diversification, 10, 134
spatial locations, of Chinese immigrant
businesses, 63–64, 135–36
spatial relocations, 134–35
spatial settlement patterns/diffusion: shift
in, 3–6; spatial diffusion of Chinese
immigrant-owned businesses, 10,
84–86, 85*fig.*
St. Louis, Missouri, Chinese immigrants
in during the nineteenth century, 4
subcontracting, 6
Sun Belt, the, 90
supply chain stores (for the restaurant
business in new destinations and
Chinatown), 119–20; 120*fig.*; James
Li's experiences in, 121–23; Tim
Chen's experiences in, 120–21

Telles, Sawyer, 98
Texas, 11, 84–86, 85*fig.*, 86, 91–92
Thailand, 45
Tina, 32–33
Toronto, 83
Trailways Bus Lines, 49
translocalism, 114
transnationalism, 114
Trillin, Calvin, 28
Tropp, Linda R., 98
Tsui, Bonnie, 143

Uber Eats, 141
US Department of Homeland Security
(DHS), 28
US Department of Transportation
(DOT), 53

Virginia, 11, 84–86, 85*fig.*, 86, 92

wages/salary: linking with immigrant
employment, 67; relation to new

wages/salary (*continued*)
destinations, 77–79. *See also* wages/salary, modeling the choices of business location and immigrant worker wages

wages/salary, modeling the choices of business location and immigrant worker wages, 68–77; distribution of jobs at the area code level, 70–71; 70*tab.*; distribution of jobs at the phone area code level, 71*fig.*; spatial models of monthly salary at the area code level, 78; variables used in the analysis of, 69–70, 69*tab.*

"Waizhou" (outside of New York City), 32

Waldinger, Roger, 18–19, 82, 91

Walter, 93

Wang, David, 49, 57

Wang, Jason, 142

Wang, Peter, 106

We-Chat groups, 11, 15, 129, 130–32

Weitzer, Ronald, 100

Wendy, 124

Wilson, W., 46, 66, 92

Yingjie, Chen, 127

Yoon, In-jin, 103, 109

Zhejiang Province, 31, 65

Zheng, Bernard, 129–31

Zheng, Lisa, 1, 3

Zheng, Lynn, 116–19; 119*fig.*

Zhou, Min, 50, 64

Founded in 1893,
UNIVERSITY OF CALIFORNIA PRESS
publishes bold, progressive books and journals
on topics in the arts, humanities, social sciences,
and natural sciences—with a focus on social
justice issues—that inspire thought and action
among readers worldwide.

The UC PRESS FOUNDATION
raises funds to uphold the press's vital role
as an independent, nonprofit publisher, and
receives philanthropic support from a wide
range of individuals and institutions—and from
committed readers like you. To learn more, visit
ucpress.edu/supportus.

Milton Keynes UK
Ingram Content Group UK Ltd.
UKHW020237200524
442884UK00005B/305